Cambridge Topics in Geography: second series

Editors   Alan R.H. Baker, Emmanuel College, Cambridge
Colin Evans, King's College School, Wimbledon

Geography, inequality and society

David M. Smith
Professor of Geography
Queen Mary College Univ

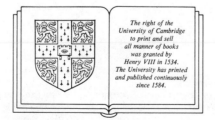

*The right of the
University of Cambridge
to print and sell
all manner of books
was granted by
Henry VIII in 1534.
The University has printed
and published continuously
since 1584.*

Cambridge University Press

Cambridge
New York   New Rochelle   Melbourne   Sydney

To my friends pictured within:

And I could wish my days to be
Bound each to each by natural piety.

(from Wordsworth's 'Intimations of Immortality from Recollections of Early Childhood')

Published by the Press Syndicate of the University of Cambridge
The Pitt Building, Trumpington Street, Cambridge CB2 1RP
32 East 57th Street, New York, NY 10022, USA
10 Stamford Road, Oakleigh, Melbourne 3166, Australia

© Cambridge University Press 1987

First published 1987

Printed in Great Britain at the University Press, Cambridge

Library of Congress cataloging in publication data
Smith, David Marshall, 1936–
Geography, inequality and society.

(Cambridge topics in geography. Second series)
Bibliography: p.
1. Equality.   2. Anthropo-geography.   I. Title.
II. Series.
HM146.S59 1987   305   87–5187

British Library cataloguing in publication data
Smith, David M. (David Marshall)
Geography, inequality and society.–
(Cambridge topics in geography. Second series).
1. Equality   2. Anthropo-geography
I. Title
305   GF41
ISBN 0 521 30477 6 hard covers
ISBN 0 521 26944 X paperback

DS

Acknowledgements
The sources for the data used in compiling the line drawings and the tables are
identified in the appropriate captions. The author and publisher would also like to thank
the following for permission to reproduce copyright material in the text: D.C. Perry and
A.J. Watkins (eds.) *The Rise of the Sunbelt Cities,* Sage Publications Inc.; K.L. Deavers
(ed.) *Alternatives to Confrontation: National Policy towards Regional Change,* Lexington
Books, D.C. Heath; G.D. Andrusz *Housing and Urban Development in the USSR,*
Macmillan, London; Nadine Gordimer *Burger's Daughter,* Jonathan Cape Ltd and the
Viking Press Inc.; the *Cape Times* and *The Sun.*

Contents

Preface

This book seeks to convey, at a fairly elementary level, some central ideas in contemporary geographical enquiry. They concern the mutual interdependence of spatial form and social structure, which finds expression through inequality in living standards. While theory, method and technique have a necessary place in any geographical textbook, there has been a tendency in recent times greatly to overdo these ingredients, at the expense of the real world experience to which the subject owes much of its long-standing popularity. The emphasis on case studies in this book is more than an attempt to capture the reader's interest; it is also a reassertion of the importance of that place-specific uniqueness which has always been a more sensitive reflection of actual human life on earth than the empirical regularities sought so assiduously during geography's recent preoccupation with statistical analysis and mathematical models.

The case studies have been chosen so as to be provocative as well as informative. In juxtaposing the United States, the Soviet Union and South Africa we consider countries constantly in the news, of which readers may already have a firm impression. That the facts and interpretations offered here may assail some preconceptions should add to the challenge of making sense of a world in which politicians, TV pundits and Sunday supplement journalists too often masquerade as serious interpreters of social reality. The cases presented here are based on more than a decade of research and months or years of living in the countries in question.

Those colleagues who have been of particular assistance in the preparation of this book will recognise my debt in the pages that follow, but some warrant individual mention: John Offord (as research assistant on a project funded by the Economic and Social Research Council), Sanford Bederman, Natasha Barbash and Denis Fair. As the interpretations in this book depart significantly from the conventional wisdom (or ideologies) purveyed in the countries concerned I hereby make it clear that they are my views alone and that some of those who helped me most may disagree most strongly.

The maps and diagrams were drawn by David Armitage and Leslie Milne in the Cartographic Unit, Department of Geography and Earth Science, Queen Mary College. Ray Crundwell provided photographic services. Sally-Anne Blake word-processed the manuscript, with assistance from Jacquie Crinnion.

Finally, thanks as always to Margaret, and to Michael and Tracey who shared some of the fieldwork and who will, I hope, understand my enigmatic dedication.

David Smith
Loughton, Essex

Introduction

Wanting to know how other people live seems a natural part of human curiosity, the more so when physical or political divides promote ignorance and even prejudice. The subject of geography was originally built on growing knowledge of a world in which ways of life were found to differ markedly from one continent or country to another. And such differences as still exist help to explain the continuing fascination and popularity of geography as a field of study, at both school and university. However, consideration of differences between places, in climate for example, soon leads to comparison of a more qualitative nature – to assertions that people are better off in one place than another. Observation thus shades into judgement, and difference becomes inequality.

It is extraordinarily difficult to demonstrate that life is better in one country (city or region) than in another. Vague assertions as to the superiority of living standards in one place require substantiation, in the form of more careful argument backed up by evidence. What is meant by 'standard of living' is clarified by reference to specific attributes, such as housing and health care, and their availability or accessibility are subject to such measurements as the number of rooms in a flat or the cost of getting to hospital and being treated. Even then there is the problem of how to balance one attribute against another, or more generally the high material living standards of the USA, for example, against the more comprehensive social services of the USSR.

This book is concerned with those differences in human life to which the term 'inequality' can be applied. It begins with an explanation of the meaning of inequality and related concepts such as standard of living, welfare and social justice, and considers how it might be possible to show persuasively if not conclusively that people in one place are better or worse off than others elsewhere (Chapter 1). It then goes on to consider alternative ways of explaining such inequalities as are observed, from traditional geographical perspectives, through more recent developments in spatial analysis, to broader contemporary interpretations grounded in political economy (Chapter 2). The USA provides a context for the further demonstration of the importance of geographical scale in the process of uneven development (Chapter 3). This leads on to a case study of the American city (Chapter 4) which is juxtaposed with a study of the Soviet city after some broader introductory material on the USSR in Chapter 5, to reveal something of the relationship between social structure and its specific manifestations in inequality under different political, economic and social conditions. Finally comes a case study of South Africa, to show, among other things, that a society popularly viewed as representing an extreme form of inequality based on racial discrimination is more difficult to understand, and to judge, than is often appreciated (Chapter 6).

The argument of this book and the manner in which it is conveyed are guided by two important tenets or principles. One might be described as philosophical in the sense that it involves a way of understanding; the other is methodological and concerns how knowledge is built up and conveyed. Both are consistent with contemporary themes in human geography, and in the social sciences at large.

The philosophical principle, at its most general, has to do with the interdependence or unity of human affairs. More specifically, it asserts that certain things to which it is customary to assign a separate identity are deeply interrelated to the point of fusing one with another. Thus geographical space is not viewed as some independent dimension within which human life is played out according to patterns imposed by society, but as integral to society such that spatial relationships are formed and re-formed in mutual interactions with the other elements (labelled economic, political, social, and so on) that characterise a society. Similarly the conventional division of geography (and science) into physical and human or social dissolves into a recognition that humankind exists in and as part of nature. Human life itself is seen as a subtle form of interaction between individuals and society, the one affecting and being affected by the other, rather than as an outcome of unconstrained human volition or of the determination of some suprahuman structure. This book, including the wording of its title, presents inequality as a crucial element in the bonding of geography and society. Inequality is a specific expression of the mutual interrelatedness of the spatial and the social, the understanding of which is advanced by the observation and analysis of both the geographical expression and the individual or group experience of inequality.

The methodological principle asserts the importance of the case study. Ever since the so-called quantitative revolution a quarter of a century ago, the practice of human geography has been preoccupied with the search for generality and almost with a disdain for the unique as the outcome of the inconvenience of human caprice or some incomprehensible random variable. This is not to say that geographical texts lacked specific cases: indeed it has become customary to scatter examples from here, there and everywhere as instances of the generalisations proposed. Most of the examples are culled from existing literature, often taken out of context, and examined with a superficiality that tends to increase with their number. The use of case studies in this book is different. Instead of offering examples of spatial patterns of inequality from many parts of the world to illustrate distance decay, core/periphery contrasts or some such generalisation, a very small number of cases have been selected as media for the exploration of themes which arise from the philosophical principle presented above, expressing particular aspects of the interrelatedness of human affairs. While some general observations may be suggested by these cases, the uniqueness of spatial-social relationships will also emerge as an important part of the story rather than as local aberrations.

The orientation of human geography has shifted with an almost bewildering frequency in recent years. School and university textbooks may suggest some stabilisation around the continuing search for generalisation, in a technically, often numerically sophisticated manner and with an expectation that the outcome will have a bearing on public policy. But there are signs of further changes, including relaxation of the mechanistic interpretations encouraged by the quantitative revolution and the age of the computer along with the resurgence of local or regional studies with their concessions to the uniqueness of place – albeit in a much broader explanatory framework. This book attempts to evoke something of these contemporary shifts in emphasis. Placing inequality centre-stage, within a scenario involving the geographer's traditional taste for case studies, brings together the contemporary concern for social relevance and our long-standing curiosity about actual places and the lives of the people who inhabit them. It is this blend of concern and curiosity which gives geography its peculiar excitement, and its resilience in a changing world.

1   Concepts and methods

For a long time the term 'areal differentiation' described the subject matter of geography to the satisfaction of most of its students and practitioners. Geographers sought to describe and explain the variable character of the earth's surface and the people living thereon. Physical differentiation was manifest in variations from place to place in physiography, climate, soils and vegetation. Differences in human life were seen largely as a locally specific response to the physical environment or resource base, which people of different cultures might appraise in different ways to generate differences in economic activity. Just as the facts of physical differentiation were synthesised in sets of physiographic provinces, climatic zones and so on, so the variable character of human activity tended to be expressed in the form of economic regions with labels such as 'cotton belt' or 'metal manufacturing region' capturing the predominant form of commodity production.

The shift of emphasis from areal differentiation to spatial organisation associated with the quantitative movement opened up a broader view of human life on earth. Geometrical form was detected in the manner in which human activity was organised and integrated in space, superimposed on the patterns of differentiation. However, the focus remained very much on economic aspects of life, with attention to social conditions largely confined to those in which some regularity of 'spatial behaviour' might be observed, measured and modelled.

The latter part of the 1960s saw the beginning of a more fundamental re-direction of human geography. The term 'radical geography' was coined to express the extent of the break with conventional wisdom as well as to evoke an orientation which had more overt social purpose than previously seen in the subject of geography. Attention came to be focused on conditions hitherto neglected as features of spatial variability in human life, including the uneven incidence of poverty, hunger, illness, crime and other manifestations of economic or social problems. The nature of these conditions and the extent to which they afflicted some people in some places more than others elsewhere provoked not only academic interest but also moral indignation and calls for remedial action. Curiosity about areal differentiation was supplemented by concern about spatial inequality as a central element in human geography.

Dimensions of inequality

Inequality is a particular kind of differentiation. People with different personal characteristics such as name, age, height, hair style or skin pigmentation are different in the sense of not being 'the same', but would not usually be regarded as unequal. The only proviso is in cases

Different – and unequal. Two of the people pictured here are of a different generation from the other two. They are also of a different race and skin pigmentation, which makes them unequal in South Africa.

where certain personal attributes are regarded socially as desirable, such as a prestigious name or a fashionable hair style, or undesirable, such as a skin colour that is subject to discrimination: then the concept of *inequality* might be invoked to portray some people as better or worse off than others. This provides an important clue to the meaning of inequality, as referring to differences which are subject to social evaluation. The point is clearer with respect to the personal characteristic of wealth: having more rather than less is so obviously desirable that it is customary to refer to differences in wealth as 'inequality'. Furthermore, such differences may be subject to another kind of social judgement: that they are too large, unjust or simply wrong.

The distinction between differentiation and inequality in a geographical context follows closely from that at the level of individuals. A cotton region and metal manufacturing region are clearly different, with respect to the predominant form of economic activity, but this cannot be regarded as inequality – unless cultivating cotton is accorded higher social standing than making metal goods. More likely, some connection with other conditions makes living in one region more desirable, for example because cotton-growing generates higher incomes than those earned from metal manufacturing. Regional differences in income clearly qualify for the description of inequalities. High regional incomes are judged better than low regional incomes, and if the degree of inequality among regions is substantial this could be a cause of moral disapproval, social concern and government action.

Unlike differentiation, inequality can provoke questions of social justice. But it is necessary at the outset to recognise that inequality is not necessarily unjust. The concept of *equity* refers to situations which are considered just, and should not be confused with equality. For example, some inequality in the distribution of income among individuals or regions may be considered justified, on the grounds of

9

differentials with respect to quantity or quality of work performed or products supplied. The crucial question is that of the circumstances in which a specific degree of inequality may be considered (in)equitable or (un)just.

An early attempt to redirect human geography towards questions of inequality and social justice introduced the catch-phrase 'who gets what where and how', to encapsulate the specific concerns of this approach (Smith, 1974). The 'who' refers to the individuals or groups whose life experiences may be unequal, the 'what' to the goods (or 'bads') which as positive or negative aspects of life are unequally distributed, and the 'where' to the territorial divisions upon which the enquiry is based. The 'how' refers to the process by which who gets what where is arrived at. Who, what and where can be regarded as the three major *dimensions* of inequality within human society at a particular point in time; that they are hard to consider without reference to how – to the process – will be apparent in subsequent discussions.

To begin with the 'who' dimension provides a reminder that there are no hard-and-fast categories that can be applied to the subdivision of a human population for the purpose of investigating inequality. Individuals differ from one another in numerous ways, and the characteristics most relevant to the understanding of inequality will depend on the nature of the society concerned. Some societies generate marked distinctions among individuals with respect to economic or political status and distribute income, goods and services accordingly. In other societies, skin pigmentation, race or ethnic origin are major distinguishing features, so that the relevant groups could be 'blacks' and 'whites' – or in South Africa the four officially recognised race groups of Blacks, Coloureds, Asians and Whites. Categories may be related, so that being black (in South Africa, or even Britain) will tend to be associated with a particular ('low') occupational and socio-economic status and with low living conditions. Identifying the most appropriate population categories for describing and explaining inequality is an important aspect of understanding the *structure* of a society, or the links binding together individuals and groups and their activities.

In some circumstances geographical location or area of residence may be relevant to the 'who' dimension, for example if some city councils are able and willing to provide superior services to others. But it is easy to exaggerate the significance of place, and hence to draw misleading conclusions from geographical patterns of inequality. Mortality rates in Britain vary regularly with social (occupational) class, so high mortality in a particular place is a reflection of the kind of people who live there rather than of the hazards to health of the place itself – though people of 'low' occupational status are more likely to live in hazardous environments. The people in South Africa's black townships like Soweto have low incomes because they are black and hence constrained with respect to education and occupation choice, not because they reside in Soweto, though once in Soweto they are subject to risks such as violent crime which are much higher than in a white area. The distinction sometimes made between 'place poverty' and 'people poverty' is crucial to the way in which the geographical and the social mesh together in mutual interaction.

The 'what' dimension of inequality has already been introduced, in suggesting that there are special criteria of differentiation, the uneven distribution of which is subject to social evaluation. These are conditions that provoke statements that it is better or worse to have more or less, as well as different. Thus by general consent it is better to have more wealth and income than less (except to those who hold unconventional views, for example that money is the root of all evil), it is better to be healthy than ill, to be educated than ignorant, secure than vulnerable. These are the kinds of conditions that we tend to associate not only with the manner or way in which we live but also with how good (or bad) it is – with *standard of living* or even *quality of life*.

Many attempts have been made in recent years to define such concepts as standard or level of living and quality of life, by lists of criteria that would elicit widespread approval. For example, in 1954 the United Nations identified the following components of 'level of living': health, food and nutrition, education, conditions of work, employment, consumption and savings, transportation, housing, clothing, recreation and entertainment, social security and human freedom. In 1973 the Organization for Economic Co-operation and Development listed the following 'social concerns' common to most member countries: health, individual development through learning, employment and the quality of working life, time and leisure, personal economic situation, physical environment, social environment, personal safety and the administration of justice, social opportunity and participation, and accessibility. The extent of overlap between the UN and OECD categories is considerable, and the same impression is gained from other lists of this kind produced by international agencies and academics (Smith, 1977, Chapter 2; 1979, 19–24).

A particularly instructive approach is that adopted by Drewnowski (1974) at the UN Research Institute for Social Development. He made a distinction between the state of welfare of a population and its level of living (Drewnowski's usage of the term 'welfare' is preserved here, though we shall suggest a different meaning later in this chapter). The state of welfare is defined in very broad terms relating to physical, mental and social conditions. Physical status refers to nutrition, health, life expectancy and fitness; educational status to literacy, educational attainment, congruence of education with manpower requirements and employment; while social status concerns integration into society and participation in its affairs. Level of living is viewed more specifically with respect to aspects of life with labels similar to those used by the UN and OECD.

Drewnoski's dual concepts incorporate a distinction between ends and means, and require the introduction of the time dimension. The state of welfare may be regarded as a broader version of the wealth of a population, with level of living as its income. Thus just as stocks of wealth are maintained (or otherwise) by flows of income, so state of welfare is maintained by level of consumption of food, clothing, shelter, and so on. The present state of a population is therefore to some extent an outcome of past levels of living. For example, present physical conditions will depend on past levels of nutrition, present mental conditions on past education received. And of course the future state of a population will depend in part on present levels of living: if they are below what is required for survival, there is no future.

Drewnowski's approach is helpful in suggesting a process of *social development*, unfolding over time. It establishes a link between inequalities past and present, which is an important element in attempts to explain inequality. It is also relevant to planning for the future, for to achieve equality of outcomes with respect to the state of a population, if this is a policy objective, may require unequal treatment with respect to items of consumption forming components of level of living. Thus to improve the state of a physically deprived population (for example, in Ethiopia) may require privileged treatment with regard to food supplies and health care to compensate for past low levels of consumption. This is a case in which inequality might be considered equitable, if it reflects differences in need to be satisfied so as to ensure equal or otherwise acceptable outcomes at some future date. Equalising levels of health in Britain requires unequal regional allocations of resources, because present conditions of the population generate greater need in some regions than in others.

There is more to the 'what' question than establishing lists of conditions which might satisfactorily define living standards or some such state. If anything precise is to be said about inequality and its patterns of incidence, relevant conditions must be subject to measurement. This requires further clarification of the meaning of health, education, leisure, and so on, and their operational definition in the form of specific numerical *indicators*. Thus health may be measured by infant mortality, education by the rate of literacy, and leisure by time free from work or other such obligations. However, it is seldom the case that the meaning of a condition is so clear as to be adequately captured by just one indicator, so the measurement of health, for example, may require recourse to a batch of mortality and morbidity rates. While conditions such as health or illness can usually be defined in a broadly if not universally acceptable manner, this is not the case with more abstract qualities of life such as happiness, liberty and human freedom (which appeared on the UN list). What is freedom to one individual, or society, may be oppression to another, and it is preferable to confine consideration of living standards to conditions less prone to political ideology and personal idiosyncracy.

The use of a multitude of indicators in studies of inequality raises a number of problems. One is how to build them into a single composite index, a taste of which is provided in the next section of this chapter. Another is that the more measures adopted the less intelligible the results may be, as information on individual conditions tends to get lost in a mass of data especially if it is subjected to sophisticated numerical manipulation. There is thus much to be said for restricting studies to a small number of carefully selected indicators. One such example is the Physical Quality of Life Index developed in the USA for the Overseas Development Council, which consists of just three indicators: life expectancy, infant mortality and literacy. The approach to be adopted in the case studies in later chapters of this book involves a limited number of crucial indicators of inequality, rather than seeking some illusory comprehensive list of life conditions and individual measures.

The final dimension in our 'who gets what where' formulation is that of geographical space or territory. Most of the attempts to generate indexes of living standards on the part of agencies such as the UN have been concerned with variations among nations. Just as conventional economic indicators such as national income or gross national product (GNP) refer by definition to entire nations, so the broader term *social indicator* usually applies to a national population. The concern of this book is almost exclusively with inequality *within* nations, as it is at the intra-national scale that the reciprocal relationship between space and society is most clearly expressed. The term *territorial social indicator* is used to distinguish measures at sub-national scales from those referring to national aggregates. The intra-national patterns of inequality revealed by territorial social indicators are an important aspect of society which tends to be obscured by the more conventional national indicators favoured by economists and other social scientists lacking the geographer's sensitivity to regional and local variations in human life.

There are various geographical scales or levels of territorial disaggregation at which intra-national studies of inequality can be undertaken. Even when choice of scale is limited by the kind of units used to compile data in official sources, as is often the case, a choice generally has to be made. In Britain, for example, data at a broad level of disaggregation of the national territory as a whole are available for counties and for the larger so-called Standard Regions, while in a metropolitan area like London there will be a successively finer breakdown from boroughs to wards and to census enumeration districts. Census figures in the USA may be available at seven different levels: four major regions, nine geographical divisions, the states, counties and (within urban counties) census tracts, enumeration districts and blocks. Data from sources other than the census may be compiled for different territorial units, which further complicates choice of spatial scale of analysis.

Practicalities of data availability aside, the answer to the 'where' question must arise from the nature of the study itself. To identify broad regional patterns of inequality in Britain would not require data on all 80,000 or so enumeration districts; at the intra-metropolitan scale data by wards would be required to reveal variations within boroughs. The importance of geographical scale in the analysis of inequality will be explored more thoroughly elsewhere in this book, where it will be shown that the degree of inequality observed varies with spatial scale and that this has an important bearing on how patterns of inequality and trends over time are interpreted.

Geographical patterns of inequality: an example from Britain

Some aspects of the practice of identifying geographical patterns of inequality in living standards may be illustrated by an example. It is sometimes claimed that Britain embodies two nations: a prosperous 'South' and a deprived 'North', the former comprising central and south-east England with its metropolitan core of Greater London, the latter being made up of the peripheral parts of Britain including northern England, Wales and Scotland. How far does such a generalisation hold up to examination in the light of evidence as to regional inequalities in living standards?

The simplest approach to this question is to take the single condition of income per capita as the most obvious criterion of living standards,

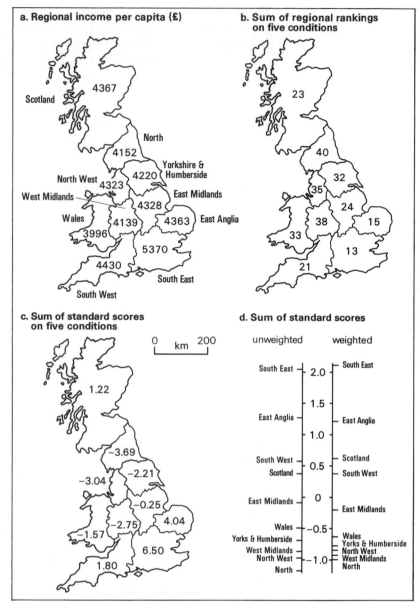

Fig. 1.1 Patterns of regional inequality in living standards in Britain, *c.* 1983. *Source*: Tables 1.1, 1.2 and 1.3.

a. Regional income per capita (£)

Scotland 4367
North 4152
Yorkshire & Humberside 4220
North West 4323
West Midlands 4328
Wales 4139
3996
East Midlands
East Anglia 4363
5370
4430
South East
South West

b. Sum of regional rankings on five conditions

23
40
35 32
38 24
33 15
21 13

c. Sum of standard scores on five conditions

1.22
−3.69
−3.04 −2.21
−0.25
−2.75 4.04
−1.57
6.50
1.80

0 km 200

d. Sum of standard scores

unweighted / weighted

unweighted		weighted
South East	2.0	South East
	1.5	
East Anglia		East Anglia
	1.0	
South West		Scotland
Scotland	0.5	South West
East Midlands	0	East Midlands
Wales	−0.5	Wales
Yorks & Humberside		Yorks & Humberside
West Midlands		North West
North West	−1.0	West Midlands
North		North

and to observe its regional variations. These are shown in Fig. 1.1a. The territorial subdivisions are the Standard Regions commonly adopted for the compilation of official statistics. The South East stands out, with income per capita well above that of its nearest rival (the South West), but to the north the pattern becomes somewhat confused with the West Midlands having a lower figure than any other region except Wales, and Scotland having a higher figure than all but the South East and South West. So there is no neat North-South distinction here.

But there is more to standard of living than monetary income, and the addition of other conditions might alter the patterns of regional inequality. Table 1.1 provides data to enable a broader view to be taken. There are five general conditions, chosen to reflect varied aspects of life that have a bearing on living standards: income, employment, health, education and crime. Each is measured by one indicator.

Although the individual indicators selected may be regarded as capturing the nature of the general condition in question in a fairly satisfactory manner, they are subject to the possibility of unreliability or error and this has to be borne in mind in the subsequent analysis. For example, published figures for personal income will exclude earnings from 'moonlighting' and other activities that evade official scrutiny; the recorded unemployment rate will exclude those out of a job but not registering as seeking work; infant mortality may not reflect adult health; staying on at school may not mean more useful education (A levels are not all that matter); and crimes reported to the police exclude much undetected business crime and financial fraud as well as those aspects of petty crime where the prospect of detection is so slight that victims fail to notify the police. Some such problems arise in any social indicators. The crucial point in the present exercise, however, is that there is unlikely to be regionally selective error – except in one particular instance. This is the education indicator where the high proportion of 16-year-olds staying on at school in Scotland reflects distinctive features of the education system when compared with England and Wales.

Table 1.1   Data for British regions on selected economic and social conditions.

Condition:	Income	Employment	Health	Education	Crime
Indicator:	Personal income/ capita (£) 1983	Unemployment rate (%) 1984	Infant deaths/1,000 live births 1983	16-year-olds in school (%) 1982-3	Offences/ 100,000 population 1983
Direction:	+	−	−	+	−
South East	5,370	9.7	9.2	31.9	6,681
South West	4,430	11.7	10.1	23.2	4,730
East Anglia	4,363	10.1	9.0	23.9	4,708
East Midlands	4,328	12.5	10.6	24.6	6,016
West Midlands	4,139	15.7	10.8	23.7	6,552
North West	4,323	16.1	10.6	24.0	7,984
Yorks. & Humberside	4,220	14.8	10.9	25.2	6,658
North	4,152	18.8	10.2	23.3	7,741
Wales	3,996	16.8	10.7	31.6	5,729
Scotland	4,367	15.2	9.9	45.0	8,703

Source: *Regional Trends* **20** (1985), Central Statistical Office.

The intention now is to use the data in Table 1.1 to generate a composite regional indicator of living standards incorporating all five conditions. The first step is to recognise the *direction* of each indicator, as shown by the sign in the table, where + means that a high positive value in the column is judged to be good and − means that it is bad. Thus high personal income per capita is good, high unemployment bad, and so on. These are judgements that could be expected to elicit widespread approval: those judging high numbers of 16-year-olds in school as bad (reluctant A-level pupils?) or high crime rates as good (criminals?) are hopefully very much the exception. The indicators chosen for a study of this kind should be as unambiguous as possible with respect to their direction.

The simplest way of combining data on different indicators, involving different units and scales of measurement, is by the use of *rankings*. In Table 1.2 ten regions have been ranked on each of the five indicators; the first or 'best' region is ranked 1 and the 'worst' 10. These ranks may then be summed, the total in the final column providing a composite indicator in which the lower the value the better the region. This is mapped in Fig. 1.1b. A comparison with the income data in Fig. 1.1a shows that there are some quite substantial changes in regional relativities. For example, Wales had the lowest per capita income but comes out better than the West Midlands, the North West and the North on total ranks. The South East is less the clear leader on total ranks than on income alone. But again, no clear North-South distinction emerges, partly because Scotland continues to compare favourably with most of the English regions.

Adding up rankings is a rather crude method of combining data, involving loss of much of the original information. An alternative frequently used in composite indicator construction is the summation of *standard scores*. The calculation of standard scores converts data on different conditions into a comparable form by standardising two basic measures of a set of numerical observations: the average or mean, and the standard deviation (roughly speaking, the average departure of individual observations from the mean). Specifically, the mean is set at zero and the standard deviation at unity, so a standard score measures departure from the mean in units of standard deviation – hence the alternative term 'standard deviates'.

Table 1.2   Rankings of British regions on selected economic and social conditions.

	Income	Employment	Health	Education	Crime	Total
South East	1	1	2	2	7	13
South West	2	3	4	10	2	21
East Anglia	4	2	1	7	1	15
East Midlands	5	4	6	5	4	24
West Midlands	9	7	9	8	5	38
North West	6	8	6	6	9	35
Yorks. & Humberside	7	5	10	4	6	32
North	8	10	5	9	8	40
Wales	10	9	8	3	3	33
Scotland	3	6	3	1	10	23

Source: calculated from Table 1.1.

The derivation of standard sources and their incorporation into composite indicators requires the following calculations, where X is a territorial social indicator for N observations (e.g. the ten regions) and Σ represents summation:

$$\text{mean of } X = \bar{X} = \frac{\Sigma X}{N}$$

$$\text{standard deviation} = \sigma = \Sigma \sqrt{\frac{(X - \bar{X})^2}{N}}$$

$$\text{or } \sigma = \sqrt{\frac{\Sigma X^2 - \bar{X}^2}{N}} \qquad \text{(this is easier to do on a desk calculator)}$$

$$\text{standard score} = Z = \frac{X - \bar{X}}{\sigma}$$

sum of $Z = \Sigma Z$, or ΣZW where W is the weighting of the indicator in question (which may be unity in all cases if there is no reason for differential weighting).

For further explanations see Smith (1975, Chapter 5; 1979, Appendix).

Table 1.3 lists standard scores for the five indicators, calculated from the data in Table 1.1. The signs are such that high positive is 'good' and high negative is 'bad'. As all five conditions are now measured on comparable scales it is easier to pick out those on which particular regions perform in a conspicuously favourable or unfavourable manner. For example, the South East rates very highly on income, East Anglia on health and Scotland on education (though the earlier reservation about the validity of this indicator in Scotland must be recalled). The highest negative ('worst') scores are for income in Wales, employment in the North, health in Yorkshire and Humberside and crime in the North West and Scotland. As well as highlighting inequality among regions on each condition, these scores (like the rankings in Table 1.2) show variations across the rows, i.e. in performance on different conditions in each region. For example, the South East does well on four conditions but drops markedly on crime, while the North does badly on four conditions but just achieves average performance on the health indicator.

However, the objective of the present exercise is not to deliberate on the varied performance of regions on different conditions, but to derive a composite index. This is done simply by summing the standard scores for each region. As a set of standard scores are balanced about the mean so that for any condition the positive and negative cancel out to total 0 (subject to rounding errors), each condition has the same overall contribution to the sum in Table 1.3 in the column under the heading 'Total unweighted'. These figures are mapped in Fig. 1.1c, to provide a third pattern for comparison. The three regions with positive sums are more clearly differentiated from the rest of England and Wales (but not Scotland) than they were by the sum of rankings: some semblance of a North-South divide can now be detected.

Once standard scores have been calculated they can be weighted differentially, to reflect differences in the importance attached to the various conditions contributing to standard of living. In the absence of any grand theory that specifies such differences, they can be arrived at only intuitively or by recourse to surveys of expert or popular opinion. As an illustration, seventy-eight students in one of the author's courses were asked to place the five conditions which are the subject of this example in order of importance to living standards, giving rank 1 to the least important and 5 to the most important. Summing the ranks given to each condition and dividing by the number of respondents produced the following average rankings: income 3.10, employment 2.92, health 4.10, education 3.12, crime 1.76. Health was thus clearly regarded as the most important, little difference emerged between income, employment and education, while crime was least important. These figures have been applied as weights to the data in Table 1.3, by simply multiplying the standard scores in the appropriate column by the weight shown. The summation of these new scales is in the column headed 'Total weighted'.

As individual regions perform differently on different conditions, the application of weights can change the relative position of regions on the composite indicator. This is illustrated in Fig. 1.1d, where regions are plotted according to sums of standard scores weighted and unweighted, where the sums have themselves both been standardised to make them strictly comparable (the two columns headed Z in Table 1.3). Not only have positions changed with weighting, but so have the order of regions. For example, Scotland and the South West have been reversed: Scotland fares better with weightings, largely because this reduces the contribution of the high crime rate to the composite indicator (crime has the lowest weight), while the South West's very favourable position on crime is diluted by the low weighting. Examination of the figures in the table will reveal explanations for other changes in the relative position of regions. Figure 1.1d shows more clearly than the maps the extent of the gaps between regions on a composite standard-of-living scale. While the idea of two nations is clearly an oversimplification, the three southern regions (with Scotland) are markedly better off than the rest. However, the gaps between regions suggest a considerable degree of inequality among the better-off, with far less inequality among the worst-off regions. The application of weightings has increased the bunching of the five regions at the bottom end of the scale, indicating that there is little to choose between them.

Applying some fairly simple numerical manipulations to indicators of five conditions thus reveals that there is more to regional inequality in Britain than a North-South dichotomy. But it must be understood that the results of this exercise are dependent on the data used – on its adequacy as an operational definition of standard of living, on its accuracy (including its absence or otherwise of regional bias) and on the way in which it has been used. That different techniques can produce different results with respect to regional relative positions, even with the same basic data, should provide a warning that the identification of geographical patterns of inequality is more difficult than might appear at first sight.

Measuring degree of inequality

The exercise just undertaken helped to establish the geographical pattern of incidence of economic and social conditions among regions but did not yield a measure of the extent or *degree* of inequality. Clearly, if all regions had the same score on the composite indicator then perfect equality would prevail: degree of inequality would be 0. How much inequality was in fact observed? We could state (from Table 1.3) that regional scores on the unweighted composite indicator ranged from 6.50 for the South East to −3.69 for the North, but this conveys little, if anything, that is useful in isolation. Degree of inequality acquires meaning only in a comparative context, in which some measure

Table 1.3 Standard scores for British regions on selected economic and social conditions.

	Income	Employment	Health	Education	Crime	Total unweighted		Total weighted	
Mean	4,369.80	14.14	10.20	27.67	6,550.20	0.00	0.00	0.00	0.00
Standard deviation	358.80	2.85	0.63	6.52	1,396.00	3.18	1.00	10.20	1.00
Weight	3.10	2.92	4.10	3.12	1.76	sum	Z	sum	Z
South East	2.79	1.56	1.59	0.65	−0.09	6.50	2.04	21.48	2.11
South West	0.17	0.86	0.16	−0.69	1.30	1.80	0.57	3.84	0.38
East Anglia	−0.02	1.42	1.90	−0.58	1.32	4.04	1.27	12.39	1.21
East Midlands	−0.11	0.58	−0.63	−0.47	0.38	−0.25	−0.08	−2.03	−0.20
West Midlands	−0.64	−0.55	−0.95	−0.61	0.00	−2.75	−0.86	−9.39	−0.92
North West	−0.13	−0.69	−0.63	−0.56	−1.03	−3.04	−0.96	−8.55	−0.84
Yorks. & Humberside	−0.41	−0.23	−1.11	−0.38	−0.08	−2.21	−0.69	−7.82	−0.77
North	−0.60	−1.64	0.00	−0.67	−0.78	−3.69	−1.16	−10.11	−0.99
Wales	−1.04	−0.93	−0.79	−0.60	−0.59	−1.57	−0.49	−6.31	−0.62
Scotland	−0.01	−0.37	0.48	2.66	−1.54	1.22	0.38	6.48	0.63

Source: calculated from Table 1.1.

for a set of regions can be compared at different points in time, for example. Or degree of inequality for different conditions in the same set of regions can be compared.

As in the case of geographical patterns of inequality, the degree of inequality observed will depend on the measurement technique adopted. Some measures are more helpful than others in capturing the relations among individual observations that compromise inequality. This can be illustrated by returning to the case of the British regions. Table 1.4 lists four alternative measures of inequality among regions, for each of the five individual indicators. The *range* of the data proves ineffectual, as the figures merely reflect the different scales on which the five conditions are themselves measured. This problem is overcome by calculating the *ratio* between maximum and minimum observations, on the basis of which it might be valid to conclude that income and infant mortality are subject to less inequality among regions than are the other three conditions. However, this ratio is based only on the two extreme values, and it can be misleading if one or both depart greatly from the rest of the data. For example, eliminating Scotland's peculiarly high figure for 16-year-olds in school reduces the ratio for this indicator to 1.36. While this ratio can be a useful summary measure of inequality if employed with care, it would be preferable to take account of all the values in a set of data. This can be done by calculating the *coefficient of variation*, which is the ratio between the mean and standard deviation, i.e. it measures the spread of observations about the mean in a manner which allows for the different scales on which conditions to be compared have been measured because dividing the standard deviations by the means holds the means constant. The coefficients of variation in Table 1.4 tend to confirm the impression given by the ratio of maximum to minimum, of unemployment, school attendance beyond 16 and crime rate subject to markedly greater regional inequality than the other two conditions. The fourth measure is the *mean percentage deviation*, which is similar to the coefficient of variation in that it identifies the spread of values about the mean or national average. In this case it is the average of the regional departures from the mean (in Table 1.3) expressed in percentages of that mean. The general magnitudes roughly confirm the degrees of inequality as measured by the coefficients of variation.

Table 1.4 Measures of degree of inequality in British regional indicators.

Measure	Personal income/ capita (£) 1983	Unemployment rate (%) 1984	Infant deaths/1,000 live births 1983	16-year-olds in school (%) 1982–3	Offences/ 100,000 population 1983
Range (max.−min.)	1,374	9.1	1.9	22.8	3,995
Ratio (max.÷min.)	1.34	1.94	1.21	1.94	1.85
Coefficient of variation	8.21	20.16	6.18	23.56	21.31
Mean percentage deviation	4.8	17.7	5.2	18.5	15.4

Source: calculated from Tables 1.1 and 1.3.

There are a number of more sophisticated methods of calculating the degree of inequality, the best known being the *Gini coefficient* and its associated graphic display as the *Lorenz curve*. They require the data in the form of percentage distributions of the attribute in question which restricts their application, but if such data are available they can be very effective descriptive devices. Take, for example, the distribution of income among the four officially recognised race groups in South Africa: the percentage of all income going to each race can be compared with the proportion of total population, as is shown in Fig. 1.2. The races are listed in order of their coefficient of advantage (i.e. percentage of income divided by percentage of population). Plotting the cumulative percentages on a graph produces the Lorenz curve. An equal distribution, where the percentage of income is the same as population, would produce a diagonal line; the further the Lorenz curve from the diagonal, the greater the degree of inequality. The Gini coefficient measures the area between the diagonal and the Lorenz curve as a proportion of the entire triangle below the diagonal: the result is 62.5 (for method of calculation see, for example, Smith, 1979, 364-5). An alternative inequality index using the same data is the coefficient of concentration, which is given by half the sum of the differences between the two sets of percentages, or 48.2. Both coefficients measure the degree of inequality on the scale 0 to 100, where 0 is perfect equality (the two percentage distributions are identical) and 100 the extreme of inequality with all income (or whatever) going to one group, or territory if a geographical distribution is involved.

Measuring the degree of inequality among geographical units is complicated by the scale problem. The difficulty of choosing the level of territorial subdivision at which to operate is aggravated by the fact that the degree of inequality in any condition can vary with the observational units adopted. This can be illustrated by infant mortality.

Deaths per 1,000 live births among nations of the world vary from 211 in Upper Volta to 7 in Sweden and Japan, according to official figures, to give a ratio of 30.1:1. Within the USA, however, variations among the nine major divisions are subject to a ratio of only 1.3:1 between the highest infant mortality in the South Atlantic to the lowest in the Pacific division. As a successively finer level of spatial disaggregation is adopted the degree of inequality increases, so that by counties in one state (Georgia) and census tracts in one city (Atlanta) the range is from about 50 to nil or virtually so. There is greater inequality among regions in Europe as a whole than within the UK; London boroughs reveal a higher ratio because there are some very low rates at this scale. The greatest inequality tends to be found among nations and among small localities, with low degrees of inequality within individual nations at a broad scale of disaggregation.

Differences in degree of inequality at different spatial scales are not simply a quirk of statistics but part of what has to be explained. They may help to reveal important aspects of process, as will be shown in Chapter 3. They are, however, an inconvenience for comparative studies, for example between nations. It might be tempting to take figures for states of the USA (ratio of 2.1 between maximum and minimum) and regions of the European Economic Community (ratio of 2.0) and assert that there is greater inequality at this level of territorial aggregation in the former than in the latter, but even if similar in size and number these territorial subdivisions are not strictly comparable. The difference between the ratios for states of the USA and regions of the EEC could be accounted for entirely by the divisions adopted. So it is extremely difficult to say that there is a greater or lesser degree of regional inequality in one country than another.

Fig. 1.2 Measuring the degree of inequality in income distribution among race groups in South Africa, 1977. *Source: Survey of Race Relations 1978*, South African Institute of Race Relations, Johannesburg, 1979.

The social significance of inequality

Having introduced the concept of inequality in its various dimensions, and explained how geographical patterns of inequality may be identified and measured, it is now necessary to consider more directly the social significance of inequality. The starting point is the distinction between equality and equity, raised earlier in the chapter. If equality is not

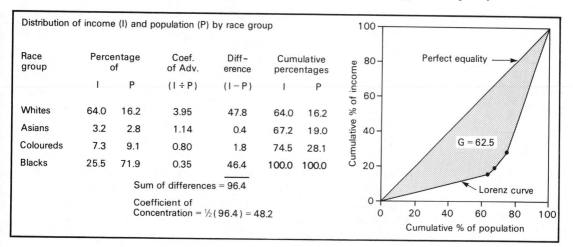

Distribution of income (I) and population (P) by race group

Race group	Percentage of I	Percentage of P	Coef. of Adv. (I ÷ P)	Diff-erence (I − P)	Cumulative percentages I	Cumulative percentages P
Whites	64.0	16.2	3.95	47.8	64.0	16.2
Asians	3.2	2.8	1.14	0.4	67.2	19.0
Coloureds	7.3	9.1	0.80	1.8	74.5	28.1
Blacks	25.5	71.9	0.35	46.4	100.0	100.0

Sum of differences = 96.4

Coefficient of Concentration = ½(96.4) = 48.2

21

necessarily inequitable, that is, it can in some way be justified, then why should inequality be a cause for concern as well as for curiosity? May inequality not perform a useful social purpose, such as encouraging those with ability to get rich by producing more wealth for the general good, or forcing the idle to work themselves out of poverty? Or is it perhaps that some degree of inequality is necessary and useful as part of a society's incentive system and an inevitable outcome of how a society and its economy functions, but that above a certain level inequality is undesirable or even dangerous?

To explore these kinds of questions requires a concept broader than that of living standard, which refers to the level of consumption or life experience. The concept of *welfare*, as used in economics, explicitly incorporates inequality in distribution in the evaluation of alternative states of society. A particular arrangement of who gets what where, in the form of the specific quantities of goods (and bads) consumed by specific individuals or population groups in specific places, carries a certain level of welfare or social approval. If things change in a particular direction, the welfare of society has improved. This may be accomplished by more goods (or less bads) being consumed, or in better combinations, or with a better distribution among individuals, population groups or territories; or welfare might be improved by a combination of any or all of these changes. Further consideration of such issues will be found in more specialised treatments of welfare and social justice (e.g. Smith, 1977, Chapter 6): the relevance of the concept of welfare to the present argument is that it firmly assigns to inequality a central place in the manner in which the general state of society is judged better or worse than some alternative state. Social justice in the sense of equity in distribution among individuals, groups or territories is an integral feature of a society, rather than an independent element to be examined or manipulated in isolation.

Welfare is one of a number of evocative terms in common usage, consideration of which assist a broader understanding of the significance of inequality. Like welfare, *social well-being* is sometimes used synonymously with standard of living or even quality of life, as something the level of which is subject to variation – that is, to inequality. Whereas the almost instinctive reaction is to attempt to define this property, just as standard of living might be defined with reference to its constituent conditions, such an approach is to misunderstand the nature of this kind of concept. It is not merely something to be tied down or boxed in by imputing specific characteristics, but a product of the human mind trying to make sense of human life in all its complexity. Such terms express an intuitive sense that things can go well or otherwise with a society. Both language and analogy are used to convey this meaning: the word 'well-being', and the analogy with a biological entity that can be well or ill. Thus the term *social deprivation* evokes falling below some accepted or expected standard (of living), but the term *social pathology* which is sometimes used to describe particular kinds of social 'problems', like crime, drug addiction and other behaviour labelled as 'deviant', conveys by its language a sense of sickness or disease threatening life itself. To put it more directly, inequality may be so great as to threaten social order, or the continuation and even survival of a society in its present form.

It is sometimes supposed that social change takes place in an orderly and deliberate manner, under the guidance or direction of governments responsive to the will of the public or the 'national interest'. New policies are introduced to satisfy unmet needs, perhaps detected by the use of territorial social indicators which, when combined with welfare evaluations, reveal a situation discordant with social justice or what ought to be. While some shifts in resource allocation may occur in this way, such a view tends to overlook the extent to which change is generated by social conflict – by the struggle of different groups in a society to gain advantage over scarce resources in situations where gains to some people, in some places, can only result in losses to others elsewhere. Those already well-endowed may have the power to retain what they have, and to keep at bay the demands of the deprived groups. In these circumstances, it may take serious threats to social order or stability to provoke change: there is nothing that sharpens the mind of governments, or those who rule, more than the violent disaffection of the ruled.

Riots have been much in the news in recent years, whether in the black townships of South Africa or the inner parts of Britain's cities. And they certainly stimulate a response, in the form of changes in government policy or in means of social control. The origin of riots is a matter of intense public debate, with their repeated occurrence in places occupied by particular kinds of people, such as those of Afro-Caribbean origin (from the West Indies) encouraging in some quarters an interpretation which portrays violence as having a racial origin. For example, shortly after the riots in British cities in 1985 one newspaper (*The Sun*) ran a feature under the headline 'THE REAL FACE OF RIOTERS' revealing the 'facts behind this year's riots', derived from a police tabulation of the type of people apprehended. 'Sixty per cent of those arrested or charged were Afro-Caribbean', it was claimed (actually 52.4 per cent), 'Four out of ten had jobs', and nearly 40 per cent were from outside the area. The fact that a group of people on the streets of Handsworth, Brixton and so on chosen at random would include high proportions of Afro-Caribbeans who happen to live there, and of outsiders who come in for entertainment, was not mentioned.

WHO WAS NICKED IN RIOTS

	HANDS-WORTH	BRIXTON	TOTT'HM	PECKHM	LEICS	TOTAL
Arrested or Charged	362	260	34	4	19	679
Afro/Carib	182	144	15	2	13	356
Asian	37	1	0	0	0	38
White	108	90	3	2	6	209
Ethnic origin unknown	35	25	16	0	0	76
Employed	131	106	1	0	0	238
Unemployed	182	126	16	0	0	324
Job unknown	42	4	15	0	15	76
Juvenile	5	24	2	4	4	39
Non-resident	127	115	11	0	0	253

How *The Sun* reported 'the facts' behind what are described as the 'race riots' in Britain in 1985.

Fig. 1.3   The spatial coincidence of social conditions and civil disorder in Los Angeles and London. *Sources*: Los Angeles map from Smith (1973, Fig. 4.2); London data from *1981 Census* (unemployment, race and housing), Inner London Education Authority (educational attainment measured by performance on verbal reasoning tests) and *Annual Abstract of Greater London Statistics* (crime) – case based in part on Fulbrook A. 'Overlapping Social Pathologies in Brixton', Independent Geographical Study, Department of Geography and Earth Science, Queen Mary College, 1985; Lambeth data from *1981 Census Data for London*, GLC, 1983.

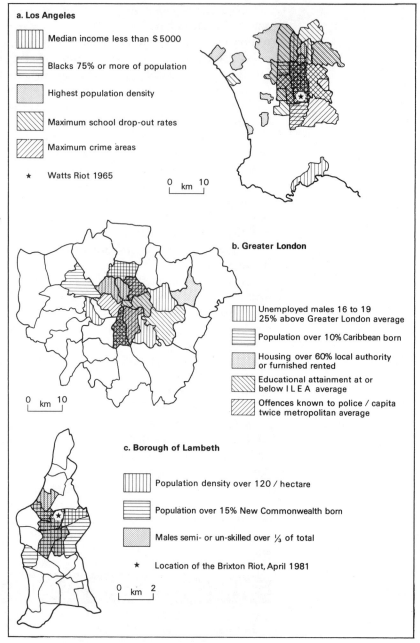

a. Los Angeles

||||| Median income less than $5000

≡ Blacks 75% or more of population

▦ Highest population density

▨ Maximum school drop-out rates

▨ Maximum crime areas

★ Watts Riot 1965

0 km 10

b. Greater London

||||| Unemployed males 16 to 19 25% above Greater London average

≡ Population over 10% Caribbean born

▦ Housing over 60% local authority or furnished rented

▨ Educational attainment at or below I L E A average

▨ Offences known to police / capita twice metropolitan average

0 km 10

c. Borough of Lambeth

||||| Population density over 120 / hectare

≡ Population over 15% New Commonwealth born

▦ Males semi- or un-skilled over ⅓ of total

★ Location of the Brixton Riot, April 1981

0 km 2

The interpretation invited was that the riots were largely the responsibility of blacks and outsiders (no doubt including 'agitators'), rather than the result of unemployment which others were putting forward as the primary cause.

If the kind of people found in areas where riots take place help to explain the location of such incidents, then more careful analyses are required. The construction and mapping of territorial social indicators provides an appropriate method, at least to begin to penetrate the problem. The worst of the riots in American cities in the 1960s was in the Watts district of Los Angeles, and it has been shown that this coincided with the worst conditions on five social indicators (Fig. 1.3a).

Applying the same method to Greater London in 1981, but with some differences in the indicators reflecting British conditions and availability of data, shows the worst conditions coinciding in the Borough of Lambeth – location of the Brixton riot in April of that year (Fig. 1.3b). At the finer spatial scale of wards within Lambeth, the highest scores on population density, population of 'New Commonwealth' origin (i.e. black, in this case mainly Afro-Caribbean) and proportion of males in the 'lowest' occupational groups of semi-skilled and unskilled work, were concentrated around the actual location of the Brixton riots (Fig. 1.3c).

Certain local population (and environmental) characteristics thus appear to be *necessary* conditions for riots, in that such outbursts occur in places with a combination of poor economic and social conditions and not in Hampstead or affluent suburbia. But they are not *sufficient* in themselves, as is shown by the fact that there were similar and indeed worse conditions in places where riots did not take place. What appeared to be sufficient conditions for a riot, at least in British cities in 1985, was poor if not the worst standard of living accompanied by a specific event involving confrontation between one or more individuals and the police, which 'sparked-off' disorders that escalated into riots. Cultural considerations may not have been entirely absent, in the sense that Afro-Caribbeans in the conditions of British inner cities may be more prone than some other groups such as Asians to violent behaviour (though those who assert some fundamental difference in this respect need only recall the violence on the Indian subcontinent at the time of independence). The significance of race is that being black in Britain, and in particular being Afro-Caribbean, is not only to be different but also to be unequal – with respect to education, employment opportunities, income and other attributes of life, the shortage of which assigns such people to areas where personal deprivation is compounded by poor housing, limited social amenities, an unhealthy environment and what is delicately described as 'a decaying urban fabric'. The problems of people and place dissolve into some broader manifestation of inequality, not confined by the boundary of the Borough of Lambeth, Handsworth, or wherever the riot happens to break out. Such conditions are an outcome of how society works. That they also feed back into society and stimulate change, for good or ill, is nowhere more obvious than in civil disorder and the response which it provokes.

Conclusion

This chapter began by discussing the meaning of inequality and proceeded to explain how its geographical expression may be identified and the degree of inequality measured. The shift of emphasis from the comfortable abstractions of welfare evaluation and social justice to the violent outcomes of what has been termed social pathology underlines the fact that inequality is more than a matter for academic speculation and analysis. Inequality is a central motivating force in society – an outcome of its operation and a source of subsequent change. The next task is to seek more systematic understanding of how inequality in geographical space arises, as a process of uneven social development.

2 Explaining inequality: alternative perspectives on uneven development

There is no single, universally accepted explanation for inequality in living standards and its spatial expression. Different disciplines tend to emphasise different causal factors, and even in the same field, like geography, alternative interpretations prevail. This chapter provides an introduction to the question of *how*, in our 'who gets what where and how', formulation, as a preliminary to more detailed examination of the interrelationships between geography, inequality and society in the case studies that follow. The intention is to review alternative perspectives on how the process of *uneven development* takes place. The concept of social development was introduced briefly in the previous chapter, to evoke a process of change unfolding over time; to couch the present discussion in terms of uneven development helps to retain a sense of social dynamics, as well as linking our concern with inequality to related issues in the broader study of development and underdevelopment.

The term 'development' is subject to a bewildering variety of meanings in academic and popular usage. Development is often taken to refer to the condition or *state* of a population defined territorially (e.g. nation or region), and in this sense may be considered synonymous with such concepts as standard of living, social well-being or quality of life. However, development also implies improvements and hence *progress*, or change in a desirable direction. Development conceived as a particular kind of change in human affairs evokes a sense of *process*, whereby different levels or states of development arise at different times and in different places. Thus uneven development manifest in a spatial pattern of inequality in living standards is the outcome of a geographically uneven process.

Three alternative perspectives on the process of uneven development have competed for attention in geography in recent years. While described here as alternatives, they are not strictly mutually exclusive. However, they do propose different basic causes of inequality in geographical space and in this sense comprise alternative interpretations of the primary relationship between geography, inequality and society. The three perspectives will be referred to as areal differentiation, spatial organisation, and political economy. The *areal differentiation* perspective is preoccupied with geographical patterns of inequality, or the state of uneven development, with explanation arising from the observed areal association of particular conditions. The *spatial organisation* perspective seeks explanation for uneven development in the spatial forms adopted by human society, as outcomes of processes which are themselves seen as manifestly spatial and embodying 'spatial behaviour'. The *political economy* perspective attempts a broader understanding of human life in its various aspects – social, economic, political, cultural and so on – as played out in geographical space and over time; it sheds light on the inequalities among individuals and groups which are also reflected in geographical patterns, and incorporates what may be thought of as specifically spatial forms and processes into a more comprehensive view of human society.

Areal differentiation

The geographer's traditional preoccupation with areal differentiation finds an obvious expression in the identification of spatial patterns of uneven development. Nations, or regions, are placed on some numerical scale, such as GNP, taken to measure the state or level of development, with the results often displayed cartographically. The underlying assumption is that territories (or the aggregates of people inhabiting them) are ranged along a continuum, with movement in one direction being progress, or development in its sense of positive change. Gaps in this continuum are a matter for concern, as indicative of the degree of inequality among nations or regions, to be reduced by accelerated development. This approach is by no means exclusive to geography; it has been influential in development studies more generally, as is demonstrated in the derivation of national indexes of development to which reference was made in the previous chapter.

This kind of approach almost invites a particular form of explanation. The most highly developed nations are observed to share certain characteristics: they are European (or populated by Europeans), with advanced capitalist economies, built on generous natural resource endowments, by energetic and ingenious people, and with democratic political institutions. Those at the bottom of the scale are predominantly in what was once described as the 'dark continent', with limited resources to facilitate economic growth, primitive or backward cultures, and in some cases burdened by dictatorships or military rule. Television coverage of catastrophes like the famine in Ethiopia encourages a view of poor nations unable to feed themselves and incapable even of organising the assistance offered by international relief agencies and pop musicians. There was a suggestion of this kind of explanation in the discussion of riots in the inner city in the previous chapter: their incidence is associated with areas of adverse economic and social conditions, which may induce violent behaviour.

The essence of the areal differentiation perspective as explanation is thus local attribution of cause and effect. The observed local (regional or national) level of development is association with local conditions, in a local process. The usual version of this interpretation is that poor nations or regions are in this state because of poor natural environment along with limited resources and/or because of some inhibiting qualities of the population such as lack of education, skills, capital, motivation or entrepreneurial ability. Geographers have traditionally been especially prone to attribute levels of living to the physical environment, and to cultural characteristics that might be associated with adaptation to it. Development is promoted when certain necessary and (it might be argued) sufficient conditions have been achieved locally, to overcome the initial disadvantages of place and/or people. There is more than an echo here of Rostow's well-known stages-of-growth theory, whereby nations move along a development continuum in stages according to the

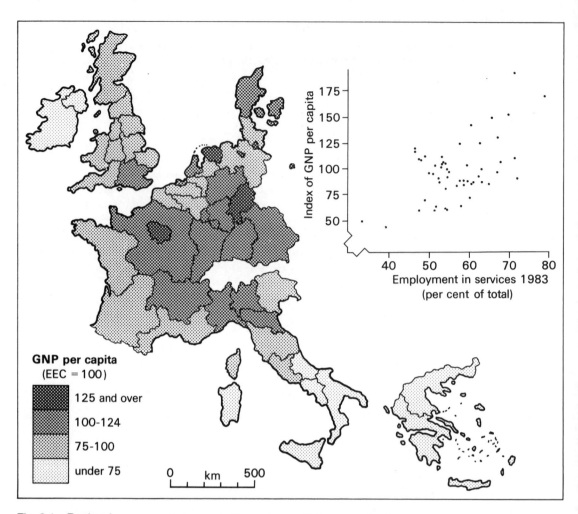

Fig. 2.1 Regional
variations in GNP per
capita in the EEC, and
their relationship with
employment in services.
Source: *Regional Trends*
20 (1985), Central
Statistical Office.

attainment of certain conditions required to progress from the initial
'traditional society' to the ultimate 'age of high mass consumption'.

To seek areal associations among conditions that might be causally
related has some intuitive appeal, especially to the geographer trained
to interpret as well as describe spatial form. That such an approach can
advance social understanding was illustrated in the example of the
urban riots. As a further illustration we may look briefly at the patterns
of uneven development in the EEC at the broad regional level at which
inequality in Britain was examined in Chapter 1. Figure 2.1 shows
differences in GNP per capita on an index where the EEC average is
100. The geographical patterns reveal a fairly clear distinction between
the *core* area with above-average GNP and the *periphery* where levels
fall to less than 75 in Ireland, southern Italy and Greece. One possible
reason for these disparities is the kind of economic activity: today high
levels of development as measured by GNP tend to be associated with
high proportions of the working population in the service sector. The
graph in Fig. 2.1 shows that the relationship of GNP per capita to
employment in services by regions is positive. Those regions with
highest index of GNP tend to have two-thirds or more of their
employment in the service sector while those with lowest GNP have less
than half and remain heavily dependent on agriculture, although in the

middle of the graph no clear association can be detected. The prescription for a more equal EEC would thus appear to be to get workers in the periphery off the land and into services, providing that enough people can pay for them.

As well as demonstrating that something can be learned from the examination of areal associations, this illustration helps to reveal limitations of this perspective. For example, the regions with highest GNP, centred on Brussels, Paris, Bremen and Hamburg, are not major concentrations of service employment simply because of some special qualities of place and people (though location was certainly relevant to the initial development of commercial functions), but because of relationships established with a hinterland or international sphere of trade. Similarly, the relative poverty of Ireland, southern Italy and Greece is not simply a matter of poor environment or 'traditional' culture (though both may constrain development), but attributable in part to an historical relationship of domination by Britain, northern Italy and Turkey respectively. Just as in the case of the inner-city riots, the sequence of cause and effect does not stop at a geographical boundary: such a view overlooks a wider system of spatial interdependence.

Core and periphery contrasts in Europe: new town of Creteil on the edge of the Paris metropolis (top); Paleochora on the south coast of the Greek island of Crete (bottom).

Spatial organisation

The basic weakness of the local attribution (and possible confusion) of cause and effect characteristic of the areal differentiation perspective is its failure to recognise the significance of connections among places: that conditions in one place (nation or region) may be largely an outcome of what happens somewhere else. The spatial organisation perspective which dominated human geography for most of the 1960s and 1970s addressed this issue, in what became a well-articulated theory which claimed not only to account for uneven development in space but also to provide a framework for its reduction via development planning. In focusing largely but not exclusively on the development process within rather than among nations, this perspective also had the advantage of recognising the internal (spatial) heterogeneity of nations, in particular those classed as underdeveloped – a view somewhat discouraged by the areal differentiation perspective with its stress on national-scale development indicators.

The main features of the spatial organisation perspective can be traced to elements of the approach to human geography built up by various pioneers of the quantitative and model-building school. Peter Haggett proposed that human activity in space could be seen as systems of nodes, networks and surfaces: nodes could represent settlements in a central-place hierarchy, networks the transportation and communication routes and flows connecting the nodes, and surfaces the spatial intensity of activity or achievement, e.g. development. The addition of the process of diffusion of innovation provided a dynamic element whereby 'modernisation' and economic 'growth impulses' spread outwards from the central metropolitan core, down the urban hierarchy, and out into the periphery. The impact on the 'development surface', identified by a multivariate analysis in the areal differentiation tradition, was that levels of development in the periphery would, over time, come more to match those of the core. The essential process was one of social transformation, whereby traditional attitudes and values would yield to modernisation in the form of the adoption of social, economic and political institutions typical of the developed (implicitly Western, capitalist) world.

What is referred to today as the 'diffusionist' paradigm attracted much interest in planning circles. It is John Friedmann (see Fair, 1982, Chapter 2; Gore, 1984, Chapter 3) who bears major responsibility for the elaboration of the spatial organisation perspective into a framework for development planning. He proposed that stages in spatial organisation could be recognised (after the fashion of Rostow's stages of growth), involving the successively greater integration of the space economy. Development could be promoted by the planned creation of 'growth points' within something approaching a central-place hierarchy which, with a well-developed system of transport and communication, would facilitate the spread of economic growth from core to periphery and thus reduce the severe disparities characteristic of most underdeveloped nations.

While some evidence could be advanced to support the diffusionist thesis, its popularity may, in retrospect, be more plausibly found in its congruence with the prevailing conventional wisdom in human geography. To combine elements of central place theory with the diffusion of innovation and the sophisticated numerical techniques usually adopted in multivariate index construction was virtually irresistible. Furthermore, the strong implication that development inequalities between core and periphery would be reduced and possibly eliminated by the natural operation of (free-market) economic forces once a properly integrated spatial structure had been created rested easily with the prediction of convergence of regional incomes embodied in neo-classical economics. These were optimistic times, with continuing economic growth generating redistributive possibilities and with faith in the capacity of careful management and planning to effect social development.

Confronted by the reality of a highly unequal world exacerbated by the mounting economic crisis of the 1970s, and of the revealed limitations of regional planning strategy actually to change it very much, it is not surprising that the diffusionist paradigm eventually attracted critical scrutiny (e.g. Browett, 1980). It was argued that modernisation or Westernisation brought costs as well as benefits, which were themselves selectively experienced under the uneven development of a capitalist economy. Doubt was expressed about the strength and reliability of the spread effect from the core or growth points. Debate was engaged concerning whether equalisation or concentration was the natural tendency in a space economy (see Gore, 1984). This extended well beyond geography and involved important questions in economic theory, beginning with Ohlin's argument that international trade would tend to equalise incomes, through Hirschman's 'trickle-down' effect which should produce the same outcome, to Myrdal's 'backwash effects' running counter to spread effects and, through a process of *cumulative causation*, encouraging concentration. At the very least it had to be recognised that the achievement of regional equality depended on something limiting further growth in the core; otherwise the periphery would never catch up.

At the heart of the limitations of the diffusionist paradigm is its tendency to abstract from economic processes and substitute superficial mechanical analogies. Thus a world was presented in which 'growth impulses', 'trickle-down' and 'backwash' purport to describe the functioning of a market-regulated economy under what was assumed but seldom explicitly recognised to be a capitalist system. What tended to be lost or obscured was that the crucial ingredient accumulated initially in the core and transmitted to other more peripheral locations was *capital*, and that capital is invested in pursuit of returns in the form of interest or profit. When these facts are placed at the forefront of the analysis an interpretation significantly different from that conventionally advanced is suggested.

This is illustrated in Fig. 2.2. At the top (a) is a summary of the conventional model, in which innovations or growth impulses spread down the urban hierarchy from the core to stimulate development in the periphery and reduce spatial income differentials. The bottom diagram (b), in contrast, indicates that the transfer of capital from core

Fig. 2.2 Alternative interpretations of the diffusion process in geographical space.

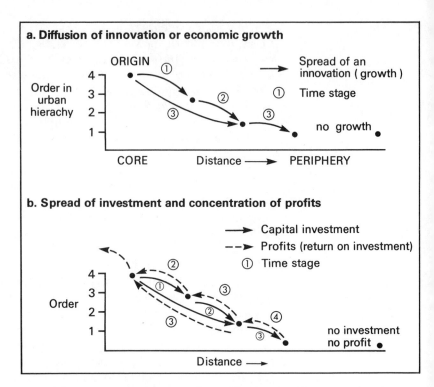

a. Diffusion of innovation or economic growth

ORIGIN

Order in urban hierachy

→ Spread of an innovation (growth)

① Time stage

no growth

CORE   Distance →   PERIPHERY

b. Spread of investment and concentration of profits

→ Capital investment

--→ Profits (return on investment)

① Time stage

Order

no investment
no profit

Distance →

to periphery generates counter-flows of returns on investment going back to the owners of capital in the core or to subsidiary centres of accumulation in the urban hierarchy or even elsewhere, beyond this nation altogether. It requires heroic assumptions concerning the mobility of capital (and other factors of production) in geographical space to generate anything other than the expectation that the nature of capital entails a continuing concentration of economic activity and attendant prosperity in the core, while not of course denying the possibility of growth in other places if and when more profitable opportunities are presented.

While the general theory of development based on spatial integration and diffusion has been found flawed, the spatial organisation perspective did shed light on the capacity of a given geographical structure of human activity to bestow its benefits (and penalties) unequally according to who they are and where they live. Distance-decay effects were observed in 'spatial behaviour', or the way in which interaction takes place, as well as in the spread of physical phenomena such as industrial pollution or noise. Thus people are advantaged or disadvantaged according to place of residence with respect to accessibility to sources of need satisfaction (e.g. shops, services, workplaces), or proximity to sources of nuisance (e.g. noxious facilities). Mathematical models made possible the identification of the optimum location for a new facility or set of facilities so as to satisfy some planning objective such as minimising total coverage of distance on the part of clients or reducing inequality of access as far as possible (see, for example, Smith, 1977, Chapter 11). However, the application of such devices requires a degree of consensus as to social objectives and a dedication to their achievements which may be discordant with the actual practice of local and national government. The real world is more often one of conflict and competition for (locational) advantage, in which resource limitations not only severely restrict residential choice for many people but also deny them the power to resist the new road, petrol station or 'development' project that may make their poor neighbourhood even worse.

Political economy

The fundamental weakness of the spatial organisation perspective is that, while recognising the importance of the interdependence of places, it largely fails to identify how this has arisen and how it actually functions under specific social, economic and political conditions. The illustration above, in Fig. 2.2b, provided a simple indication that certain things follow from the nature of capitalism: for example, that capital is invested for profit and that payment of returns involves a transfer from one place to another. To be more specific, when capitalists in the core invest profitably in the periphery, some of the value of goods thus produced in the periphery by local labour is transferred back to the core. If land in the periphery is owned by people living in the capital city – which is often the case in underdeveloped countries – then part of the product of labour working that land will end up in the city as profit or rent. And even if there is local ownership of capital and land in the periphery, this is no guarantee that profit and rent will be reinvested locally: there may be more profitable opportunities elsewhere. Similarly, the spatial arrangement of residences, workplaces, social facilities and so on in cities reflects power in the market-place or whatever device allocates scarce resources such as land among alternative uses, which is a social construct not a universal mechanism.

The political-economy perspective seeks fundamental understanding of the operation of an economic system and its associated political and social structure. Its application in geography (and in other disciplines) is almost entirely confined to the workings of capitalism, but it is just as important to understand socialism – under some form of which over 1,500 million of the world's people live. Whereas the spatial organisation perspective tends to portray an economic system as a mechanical device or set of technical relations somehow taken as given, the political-economy perspective emphasises the social relations manifest in economic activity (i.e. between capitalists and landowners on the one hand and labour on the other) and the fact that they are historically and spatially specific creations of human practice.

The crucial distinctions between different forms of human society may be explained briefly by reference to an account of social structure and the process of social development at its most general (Fig. 2.3). Human existence in a physical sense requires the production of whatever is needed at least to keep people alive. Production involves the application of human labour to natural resources, usually via the intermediary of instruments (which may range from a digging stick or hunting knife to an oil refinery or steel works). The objects on which labour is expended along with the means of so doing are known collectively as the *means of production*. Human labour together with

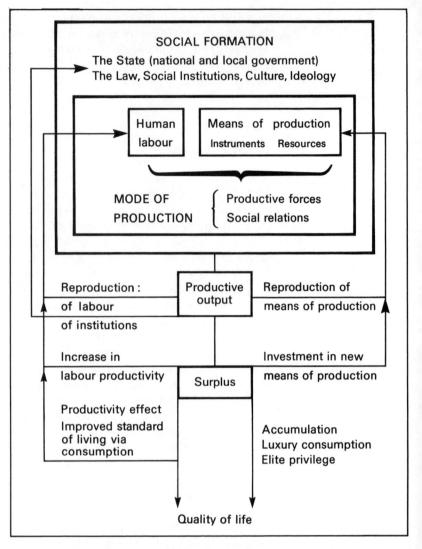

Fig. 2.3 An outline of the process of social development.

the means of production comprise the *productive forces*, or the technical capacity to produce, which may be brought together in various ways, e.g. labour-intensive production or capital-intensive with sophisticated equipment. These are the technical relationships, whereby so-much productive output is achieved by particular ways in which the ingredients or inputs of labour, instruments (or capital equipment) and resources are combined. And this of course entails a specific spatial form.

In addition, any process of production has *social relations* connecting the various human participants and differentiating their roles. It is in these social relations that fundamental distinctions are to be found: for example between slavery in which some people (who provide most of the labour) are actually owned by others, capitalism in which some (few) people own the means of production in the form of capital equipment and land with its natural resources, and socialism in which the means of production are collectively owned. The term *mode of production* describes a particular set of social relations, with which is associated a certain level of development of the productive forces. Thus feudalism involves labour bound to landowners and masters by various obligations, often of a non-pecuniary kind, in a manner which constrains the technical capacity to produce; that is, it is rather inefficient. Under capitalism labour is bound to those who own the means of production only by the employment contract, and is free to sell its capacity to work to the highest bidder just as capital can be allocated to activities offering the highest profit, all of which facilitates the development of the productive forces; that is, it is an efficient way of producing more from limited labour and resources. Just as the manner in which production is undertaken technically can vary from place to place, so can the social relations.

But a society cannot be described solely by its prevailing or predominant mode of production. Different capitalist societies have different institutions: for example, Britain has a monarch and a National Health Service, the USA has a President and predominantly private medical practice; South Africa deprives those who are black of the franchise, the USA no longer does this, and Britain never has – though property ownership and male gender were once necessary qualifications. Socialist societies also differ: no individual may legally employ another in the USSR, whereas some private business involving payment for the labour of others is permitted in Poland. The term *social formation* refers to the specific form of a society, including its perhaps distinctive state apparatus, legal system, other insitutions such as social services, culture and prevailing ideology or set of beliefs which help people to make sense of their existence and come to terms with it (or otherwise, if 'dissidents'). Differences in the social formation may exist at a regional and local level as well as among nations, and are important to the actual practice of societies under a given mode of production. For example, attitudes in parts of the American South permit treatment of black people that would be unacceptable in more 'liberal' northern states. Some parts of Britain have a tradition of labour militancy; in others workers seldom strike.

The form or structure of a society also includes the way people may be bound together in groups or *classes*. These may be defined by common interest and purpose as well as by economic status as worker or capitalist, peasant or landowner. Other ties that have a bearing on human association and practice include those of family, workplace and neighbourhood or local community, the relative strength of which can vary with the social formation as well as the mode of production.

Having identified the main features of the structure of human society we may now introduce a dynamic element, to elaborate the concept of social development. The first imperative of any society is survival, to ensure its own reproduction in a physical sense, and this is the first call on what is produced (Fig. 2.3). Labour has to be reproduced, by having enough food, clothing, shelter and so on to continue to exist and to contribute to further production, and also in the sense of having conditions conducive to its ongoing reproduction from one generation to another. The means of production used up in one round of output also have to be reproduced if further output at the same level is to be assured; this applies not only to capital equipment that has been depreciated but also to finding a replacement for non-renewable natural resources that have been depleted. The survival of a society in its present form also requires the production of the state institutions and so on required for organisation and control, including whatever maintains the prevailing social relations of production and the set of beliefs that help to hold a society together. For a society just to maintain survival or its present standard of living is termed *simple reproduction*.

The generation of production surplus to what is required for simple reproduction enables *expanded reproduction* to take place. The productive capacity of labour can be increased by improving physical fitness through better diet, housing and health care, or improving skills through the provision of more education and training facilities. Surplus production can also be devoted to investment in new means of production, research and technical advances, further to enhance the physical capacity to produce, and this can of course involve new locations and hence changes in spatial organisation. Other ways in which the surplus can be used include measures to raise living standards by increasing the output of goods and services which improve quality of life without necessarily making people more productive. For a society to reproduce itself in this expanded form may be regarded as social development.

However, to consider any kind of expanded reproduction as development in the sense of change for the better is by no means straightforward. To judge one state of society as an improvement on another involves consideration of who is better off where, as well as recognition that the volume of goods and services has been increased, as was explained in considering social justice and the concept of welfare in Chapter 1. Depending on the nature of the society concerned, the surplus may be deployed predominantly to enhance the living standards of the mass of the people, or it could be appropriated by a small elite further to promote their own privileges or luxurious lifestyle. Not even an increase in the overall value of goods and services produced is unambiguously for the better, as some combinations may be preferable to others. There may be an impetus within the system to concentrate on particular lines of output (such as sophisticated electronic gadgetry or weapons) to the exclusion of others (such as improved education or health care) that might satisfy a different kind of human need. Expanded output is not necessarily used to improve the lives of people in the places most in need, such as the famine belt of central Africa, the peripheral regions of Europe or Britain's inner cities. Expanded reproduction does not necessarily reduce inequality, personally or geographically.

Except in societies only just able to survive or producing very little surplus, the disposal of additional output is a matter of controversy and often conflict. Different individuals and groups, in different localities, will deploy whatever power is at their disposal in a struggle for advantage with respect to who gets what where. The struggle is seldom as simple as the class conflict between labour and capital which some see as the basic force for change in capitalist society – though the unequal power relations between labour, however well organised, and capital backed by the state are important elements in the structure of such societies. More often it is a case of interest groups forming around specific issues, such as defence of local services, opposition to neighbourhood redevelopment, the promotion of interests of particular occupations and industries, and so on. These issues will themselves have arisen from strains, tensions or *contradictions* within the societal structure, such as the contradiction between downward pressure on wages to reduce labour costs in the interest of profits and the need for workers to have enough money to buy the products, the sale of which realises profit. The resolution of such conflicts will set in motion further changes, including the spatial form of human activity. When, and where, conditions become intolerable, conflict can take on violent dimensions, as in some strikes and inner-city riots. At the extreme, if the existing social structure is quite incapable of responding to demands placed upon it in reconciling contradictory or conflicting forces – if ongoing reproduction in its present form is no longer sustainable – then revolutionary change can occur. Such was the case in Russia in 1917. Such may be the case in South Africa in the not-too-distant future. To some people, possibly the vast majority, this may be social development.

While the discussion has concentrated on broad features of social structure and the process of social change or development, it is important to recognise the role of individuals. Human society is more than a macro-scale structure driven on by its reproductive imperative and by the outcome of group conflict. Individuals can play a crucial role, especially at crucial times and in crucial places. It took someone like Lenin to forge opposition to Tsarism into a successful revolution. Opposition to apartheid in South Africa is crystallised by particular individuals such as Nelson Mandela. Social stability and social change both require individuals to recognise features of the structure within which they live, reconciling themselves to it or otherwise. The structures are themselves products of conscious human action, and they continue or change according to how individuals as well as groups or classes respond to them. Thus *human agency* as individual volition and action must be seen as integral to social structure and development. People are more than merely passive beneficiaries or victims of forces entirely beyond their control, just as geographical space is an integral active agent in human affairs and not just a blank map on which society imposes spatial form.

Uneven development under capitalism

The geographical dimension remained deliberately muted in the previous section. It must now be resurrected in the specific context of the political-economy perspective. This will be done by briefly considering the process of uneven development under capitalism, which has been the subject of extensive recent investigation and debate. Such a discussion provides background for the first of the detailed case studies – of the USA. Consideration of uneven development under socialism is reserved for the case to be presented in Chapter 5.

Capitalism is intrinsically competitive, and those who own means of production must continually make profits in order to survive. Production is more profitable in some places than others: the forces of production in the form of human labour, natural resources and existing means of labour (including capital equipment and social infrastructure) are better developed in some places than others. Capitalism is also expansionary, in the sense that if profit-making opportunities have been exhausted in one place they must be sought elsewhere if further profits are to be made. Thus additional (or cheaper) labour, materials and so on may be brought in from another region or nation, or utilised where they are actually found by taking capital to them. Similarly, if local markets are saturated, other customers must be found if commodities are to continue to be sold and profit realised. All this requires systems of transport, trade and communications, and organisation to ensure reliable supplies of labour and means of production and disposal of what is produced. Such a process of spatial expansion and integration is largely responsible for the present form of the world economy, and its state of uneven development. A world of differences in ways of life has been largely replaced by uniformity of the conditions under which production takes place; that is, in the level of development of the productive forces, as modern technology has diffused across the globe. But the benefits are unequally experienced, internationally and within nations.

This skeletal interpretation may be fleshed out as follows. The present interdependence and inequality among nations may be traced back to the expansion of Western European capitalism, as new investment opportunities, materials and markets were sought overseas. Settlement led to colonisation and imperialism, with European nations exercising political control over those parts of the world which became extensions of their domestic economies. The economies of the colonised lands became geared to the (external) needs of the colonisers, and selective with respect to lines of output as they became specialised producers of what were often just a few commodities for export. As the 'modern' sector of the economy grew, the indigenous system of production and social structure was broken down, exacerbating uneven development. Rural poverty set in motion migration to the cities, thus accentuating the process of concentration of economic activity. At a broader scale a similar process was taking place, with the emergence of a world core/periphery structure characterised by a dependent and exploitative relationship between the advanced capitalist world (core) and the periphery of underdeveloped nations.

As political independence has been achieved by most of the ex-colonies, a form of 'neo-colonialism' has occurred. Direct political rule has been replaced by economic control, increasingly exercised by major trans-national corporations. With this has come a new form of domination, with the USA in particular attempting to ensure the continuation of regimes conducive to the interests of American capital (for example in Central and South America). The crude notion of nations dominating or exploiting other nations has been replaced by a recognition of trans-national class alignments, whereby an indigenous elite of local capitalists, landowners, government, military and corporation functionaries has arisen. This group is markedly differentiated in economic status from the mass of the people, for whom wage labour is an increasingly elusive best prospect and for a growing number of whom the informal sector in the squatter settlements of the cities is a tenuous source of a livelihood denied by the modern sector. The widening class inequality in such nations usually follows and exacerbates the core/periphery distinction, but with rural poverty now being transferred on a large scale to the squatter settlements, creating a more diversified and unequal metropolis.

It is important to recognise that the political-economy intepretation by no means renders irrelevant the areal differentiation and spatial organisation perspectives. It does, however, place them in a new context. To understand the nature and extent of uneven development among and within nations, its origins in the process of capitalist expansion and integration must be understood. And spatial organisation is seen as intrinsic to this functioning, with each nation having a spatial economic structure consistent with its role in the broader structure involving specialisation within the international division of labour.

Recent studies have emphasised the mutual interdependence of space and society under capitalism. For example, Massey (1984) uses the concept of *spatial structures of production* to incorporate not only production techniques but also aspects of social (class) relations. Different spatial structures of production generate distinct effects on particular regions, which feed back into the process of change. Thus one region with its traditional industry in decline may be attractive to new activities because cheap un-unionised female labour may be available, while another may be avoided by capital because of its history of strong class identity and labour militancy. Massey refers to successive 'layers of investment', as old spatial structures are reorganised or replaced in response to the profit-making opportunities for new activities provided by what has gone before. Similar suggestions have been made by Smith (1984), who sees the world as a 'profit surface' generated at the global, national and urban scales by capitalist production: capital moves over this surface, developing areas where the rate of profit is high and abandoning or 'underdeveloping' those where it is low – which may themselves subsequently become attractive to capital as sources of cheap labour, for example, and hence of further profits. Capital attempts to 'see-saw' from one region to another as conditions change, in its perpetual search for profits. The state of uneven development or inequality in living standards at any point in time reflects the particular stage in the process of uneven development.

Conclusion

We have reached the point at which further generalities can contribute little more to the understanding of inequality. What is now required is to see how inequality arises in specific situations, in case studies that can help to reveal not only features of general processes of uneven development under capitalism (and socialism) but also some of the details of the interdependence of space and society arising from the uniqueness of place and of the people there at particular times. This is the task of the remainder of the book.

3 Regional inequality in the USA: a question of scale

This chapter provides a broad analysis of inequality in the USA, at what is for convenience described as the regional scale. It proceeds from a review of national patterns of inequality to the evidence for convergence of incomes, which leads on to an outline interpretation of the process of uneven development. The focus then shifts to the intra-regional scale, with an examination of the South, in order to penetrate regional patterns in more detail and to provide a prelude to the study, in the next chapter, of one major southern city.

The case to be presented contains specific applications of methods and approaches explained in the first two chapters. The identification of patterns of inequality and the measurement of degree of inequality rests on some of the technique covered in Chapter 1. The interpretation of uneven development invokes aspects of the areal differentiation, spatial organisation and political-economy perspectives explained in Chapter 2. Particular emphasis is placed on the question of geographical scale, to show not only that the pattern and degree of inequality changes with scale but also to suggest that different though related processes operate at different scales. Scale is thus shown to be intrinsic to the interrelationship between space and society expressed through inequality in living standards.

Patterns of inequality

Inequality in geographical space may be identified at a number of alternative scales in the USA. In so far as the compilation of territorial social indicators depends on government statistical sources, the broadest scale is that of the four official 'regions' of the West, Midwest, Northeast and South. While even at this scale inequality can be observed (e.g. personal income per capita is higher in the Northeast and West than in the Midwest, with the South having the lowest levels), these areas are so large and subject to such internal variations that they are unsuitable even for introductory purposes. The starting point will therefore be the nine official census 'divisions', comprising groups of contiguous states with greater homogeneity than exists within the four regions.

Table 3.1 provides measures on five economic and social indicators for each of the divisions. In order to retain some international-comparative perspective the conditions chosen are the same as in the illustration involving the ten standard regions of Britain in Chapter 1, though the actual indicator used differs for education (compare Table 1.1). As with the British regional data, that for divisions of the USA shows some inconsistency in both pattern and degree of inequality. The rankings suggest that crime is the most deviant indicator: the lowest-

Table 3.1 Economic and social indicators for divisions of the USA.

Division	Personal income/capita ($) 1983		Unemployment rate (%) 1983		Infant deaths/1,000 live births 1981		Population completing high school (%) 1980		Crimes/100,000 population 1983		Sum of ranks
USA	11,675		9.6		11.9		66.5		5,159		
New England	12,845	*2*	6.8	*1*	10.5	*3*	70.5	*3*	4,717	*3*	*12*
Middle Atlantic	12,804	*3*	9.4	*6*	11.9	*5*	66.0	*6*	4,884	*4*	*24*
East North Central	11,599	*4*	12.0	*8*	12.6	*7*	67.3	*5*	5,052	*5*	*29*
West North Central	11,242	*5*	7.9	*2*	11.1	*4*	69.6	*4*	4,090	*2*	*17*
South Atlantic	11,020	*7*	8.5	*3*	13.6	*9*	61.3	*8*	5,109	*6*	*33*
East South Central	9,056	*9*	12.3	*9*	13.2	*8*	55.3	*9*	3,753	*1*	*36*
West South Central	11,173	*6*	8.9	*5*	12.1	*6*	61.5	*7*	5,413	*7*	*31*
Mountain	10,864	*8*	8.6	*4*	10.4	*2*	75.2	*1*	5,884	*8*	*23*
Pacific	12,920	*1*	9.9	*7*	10.3	*1*	74.3	*2*	6,531	*9*	*20*
Max.÷min.	1.43		1.81		1.32		1.36		1.74		

Note: Numbers in italics are ranks, from 1 for 'best' division to 10 for 'worst'. The divisions are defined in Fig. 3.1.
Source: *Statistical Abstract of the United States*, 1985 (US Department of Commerce, Bureau of the Census).

crime division is East South Central which is bottom on all other indicators except infant mortality where it is next to bottom, while the highest-crime division, Pacific, ranks 1 on two indicators and 2 on another. Looking across the rows, some regions perform consistently – New England, for example – while others, like Mountain, show marked variations in rankings. A simple measure of degree of inequality (maximum value divided by minimum) shows unemployment and crime subject to greater inequality among divisions than the other three indicators.

Despite the inconsistencies referred to above, the data in Table 3.1 do provide a first indication of a pattern of spatial inequality. The summation of the five sets of ranks show New England to have the highest overall living standards, followed by the West North Central division. Three others – Pacific, Mountain and Middle Atlantic – come next, close together, with a gap separating them from the final four of which East South Central is worst-off overall. The general trend is thus for living standards to fall from the north and west to the south and east.

To fill out this broad generalisation requires another change in geographical scale – to the states. It is at this level that most investigations of regional variations are conducted in the USA. This is partly because the forty-eight coterminous states provide a fairly detailed depiction of geographical patterns, partly because most data are available at this scale, and partly because the states have sufficient political autonomy that actions of their governments can have a significant impact on the living standards of their inhabitants in certain respects. Figure 3.1 is based on the five indicators used in Table 3.1, with the states ranked on each measure and then re-ranked according to the sum of their ranks. There is a marked concentration of the bottom ten states in the south east, separated by a zone of intermediate states from those with highest standards of living in parts of the plains and upper mid-west along with a section of the north-eastern seaboard.

41

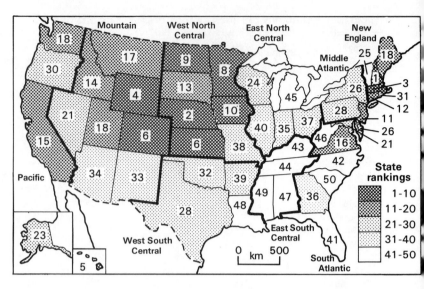

Fig. 3.1 State rankings on a composite indicator of living standards, based on indicators in Table 3.1. *Source*: data from *Statistical Abstract of the United States*, 1985.

As the USA is so highly urbanised it would not be surprising if inequality in living standards among cities revealed a similar pattern to that at the state level. That this is so is demonstrated in an extensive literature (Smith, 1973; Cutter, 1985). Despite the variety of data and methods used, the patterns revealed when city scores are mapped do confirm those by states: living standards in US cities fall fairly regularly towards the south-eastern corner of the country.

A comparison between data for states and cities does show one important difference, however: in the degree of inequality. Just as the nine major divisions are subject to internal (inter-state) variations, so it is within the states, and this is expressed at the city scale where more of the extremes are revealed. Table 3.2 indicates the range of the five measures already used in Table 3.1 and Fig. 3.1, along with the ratio of maximum to minimum values, by states and by the 300 or so Standard

Table 3.2 Degree of inequality in economic and social indicators in the USA by States and Metropolitan Areas.

Indicator	States			Metropolitan Areas		
	Maximum	Minimum	Ratio	Maximum	Minimum	Ratio
Personal income/capita($) 1983	16,820	8,072	2.08	19,020	6,012	3.16
Unemployment (%) 1984	15.0	4.3	3.49	21.1	3.0	7.03
Infant deaths/1,000 live births 1981, 1978	16.1	7.7	2.09	28.1	5.7	4.93
Population completing high school (%) 1980	82.5	53.1	1.55	not available		
Crimes/100,000 population 1983, 1980	6,781	2,419	2.80	11,582	1,887	6.24

Sources: Statistical Abstract of the United States, 1985 and State and Metropolitan Area Data Book, 1982, 1986 (US Department of Commerce, Bureau of the Census).

Metropolitan Statistical Areas. Although data on the educational indicator are not available by metropolitan areas, the other four show a marked increase in the degree of inequality when compared with the states, according to the ratio of extremes. And if these are compared with the same ratio by divisions in Table 3.1 the trend is clear: degree of inequality increases with geographical disaggregation.

The process of uneven development

We have proceeded thus far on the assumption that there is more to standard of living than monetary income, generating composite indicators to reveal geographical patterns and using multiple criteria to measure degree of inequality. However, in shifting from description to explanation it is more convenient to confine attention to the single criterion of income. While some inconsistency of performance of territories on different criteria has been recognised, income has been shown in numerous studies to be the best surrogate for standard of living more broadly defined. Furthermore, the historical perspective required to examine the process of uneven development means that other data are often less reliable than measures of income, and it is in terms of income that the debate on trends in regional inequality has, for the most part, been conducted. The present pattern of inequality in income per capita among the states is little different from that in Fig. 3.1: low-income states are concentrated in the south-east, while the highest incomes are found, less continuously, in the north and west.

Three alternative perspectives on the process of uneven development were suggested in the previous chapter. Each will play a part in the interpretation to be presented here, but at successively more fundamental levels. The areal differentiation perspective has some light to shed, for the concentration of high- and low-income states can be shown to be associated with other regional characteristics. For example, high incomes tend to predominate in the major manufacturing belt extending from New England to the mid-west, and the south-eastern concentration of low incomes closely corresponds with the old cotton belt. But to focus on these associations risks the superficiality to which traditional geographical approaches are so prone. The spatial organisation and integration of the economy must be considered, in historical perspective and within a framework of political economy which recognises certain crucial features of the prevailing capitalist mode of production and its distinctive social formation in the USA. Only thus can we begin to understand the interaction of space and society which has generated the present pattern of inequality.

A convenient starting point is provided by the long-standing debate on convergence of regional incomes. The conventional wisdom in (regional) economics is that a competitive free-market economy of the kind assumed to exist in the USA has a natural tendency towards the equalisation of incomes in geographical space. Labour and capital will move to those places where they can earn the highest wages and profits; returns will be reduced as the local price of labour and capital increases in relation to demand, until better prospects elsewhere set in motion further locational adjustments. A state of equilibrium will eventually be reached in which no advantage is to be derived from further movement, as wages and profits have been brought to the same level everywhere by the process of competition. Any subsequent change, such as in local labour supply or the discovery of new mineral resources, will set in motion an automatic process of locational readjustment until regional incomes are equalised again as equilibrium is restored. Spatial organisation assists this process, with efficient and well-integrated transport and communication systems facilitating the mobility of labour, materials, capital and innovation on which the equilibrating and equalising mechanisms depend.

An alternative view is that an economy is, in fact, in a constant state of disequilibrium, with natural resources as well as labour and capital insufficiently mobile to adjust to recurrent changes. Places that achieve early prosperity, possibly because of favourable resource endowment, tend to retain and enhance their advantage, by the process of cumulative causation identified by Myrdal to which reference was made in the previous chapter. Increasing concentration of economic activity will tend to perpetuate and exacerbate a particular pattern of uneven development, reflected in marked inequalities in regional incomes and general living standards.

The actual experience of the USA provides what at first sight may seem strong support for the equalisation thesis. For example, the economist J.G. Williamson, whose name is closely associated with the regional convergence thesis, has demonstrated a steady reduction in income inequality among regions (divisions) and states from 1880 to 1960, interrupted only by the depression in the 1920s and 1930s (see Smith, 1977, Fig. 10.11). The extent of regional convergence during the present century is shown vividly in Fig. 3.2, in which per capita income in each division is plotted as percentage of the national figure. The mean percentage deviation is indicated for each of the years plotted, to provide a more sensitive measure of degree of inequality than the ratio

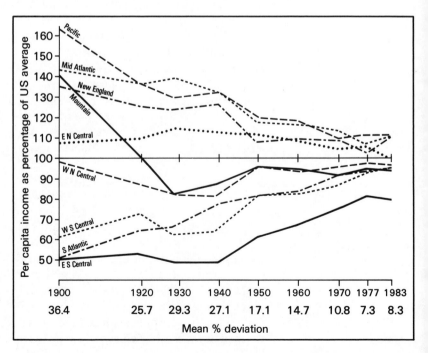

Fig. 3.2 Convergence of per capita incomes in the USA by divisions, 1900–83. *Source*: Estall (1980), Fig. 2, updated.

44

of extreme values. This figure decreases dramatically, except for an upturn associated with the depression of the 1920s and 1930s and a slight increase in the most recent figures, perhaps associated with the current recession (downturns in national prosperity often have the most severe impact on the poorest regions).

An important feature of Fig. 3.2 is that, despite the general convergence trend, divisions with the highest positive deviations in income at the beginning of the century have preserved their position, for the most part, and the same appears true at the lower end of the scale. For example, the top (Pacific) and bottom (East South Central) are the same in 1900 and 1983. This suggests a process consistent with cumulative causation. However, a close examination of the graph reveals some significant changes in relative standing, most dramatically in the case of the Mountain division's steep fall early this century and the steady improvement of income levels in the South Atlantic relative to some other divisons. Clearly, the changing pattern of regional development involves more than simple convergence modified by elements of cumulative causation.

To account for what has been observed requires an interpretation more consistent with actual historical experience. The nation was formed under conditions where the competition intrinsic to capitalism was heightened by the struggles in which people had to engage, whether with an often hostile environment and indigenous population or with others seeking a living in a new land, and this has made for a volatile process of development rather than some bland tendency towards equilibrium. And it has not been simply a case of initial advantage generating further and continuing advantage, for the major beneficiaries of economic growth have shifted over time, both regionally and within the system of cities. It is more a matter of distinct stages of development, each one laying down its own spatial form which is subsequently reappraised as conditions for profit-making change. In Massey's terms, another layer of investment responds to a new geography of comparative economic advantage, which feeds back into the process of subsequent change. Or in the words of Neil Smith used in the previous chapter, capital see-saws from one region to another according to these changing patterns.

An interpretation of uneven development in the American urban system along these lines is summarised as follows by Perry and Watkins (1977, 15–16), who see new phases associated with distinct stages of capital accumulation:

New cities emerge by capturing a significant proportion of the new dynamic activities spawned within each stage while the other cities remain locked into old economic activities, thus limiting their abilities to capitalize on the requirements of the new epoch . . . uneven development results from a shifting array of barriers and opportunities generated by each epoch. Specifically, those cities which are rapidly ascending the urban hierarchy protect their dominant position by establishing a set of institutional and structural barriers which limit the number of competing centres. As a result, the subordinate metropolitan areas serve as colonial appendages, producing wealth which primarily benefits the dominant urban areas. However, as the existing era wanes, the addiction to the old methods

45

and practices becomes a barrier blocking further growth in the dominant centres. The formerly subordinate cities, by dint of their peripheral position in the old epoch and their lack of attachment to the old economic activities, are perfectly suited to capitalize on the opportunities generated by the new wave of capital accumulation. In this way, the mantle of growth is continuously shifted from one region to the next and the result is a pattern of uneven regional development.

Three stages are recognised in the elaboration of this interpretation: the commercial or mercantile phase, the industrial or manufacturing phase, and the post-industrial phase (corresponding with the period in which the economy of the USA ceased to be dominated by manufacturing). Each responded to the spatial form which it inherited, and partially reconstructed it to serve the needs of the new era. Thus are geography and society inextricably linked, in the process generating and reacting to specific patterns of inequality.

The *mercantile phase* followed the initial period of local self-sufficiency of the early settlements and the life of the frontier. As the nation and its economy became more integrated spatially, the emphasis shifted to exploitation of fixed natural resources for more extensive markets. The most rapid growth was where newly-discovered sources of minerals were opened up, exemplified by the highly localised and often transient prosperity of the mining towns of the west. Thus by 1880 income per capita in the Far West (211 per cent of the national average) and the Mountain region (166) had outstripped the earlier settled regions of New England and the Mid-Atlantic (both about 140) and were far ahead of the largely agricultural plains and south (figures from Fox, 1978, Table 1). Trading in commodities was the major source of profits in the mercantile phase; New York, as the emerging financial centre of the nation, gained a growing competitive advantage over the other leading ports of the colonial era (Boston, Philadelphia and Baltimore), and new commercial centres began to emerge in the plains and on the west coast.

As the subsequent *industrial phase* of development gathered strength during the second half of the nineteenth century, new growth points appeared. They were partly an outcome of the localisation of materials, as in the coal, iron and steel towns of Pennsylvania, or of local sources of power such as the New England rivers which drove the early textile mills. But the geographical selectivity of capital investment in manufacturing also reflected failure on the part of the established mercantile centres to respond to new opportunities. Their commitment to older industries, often processing local materials or with largely local markets, created barriers to further development, and the newer growth industries settled in other places in the manufacturing belt. These industries were characterised by fewer and larger organisational units, increasingly less responsive to local features of natural resource endowment and serving national rather than local or regional markets. The city of Detroit, dominated by the motor industry and its few major corporations, was the ultimate achievement of the industrial phase.

The south east gained substantially neither from the mercantile phase nor from the industrial era which replaced it, and this was reflected in the very low levels of per capita income relative to other regions (half

A Montana 'ghost town', one of the last century's growth points abandoned by capital when the ore became unprofitable to mine.

the national average in 1900). The evolving transportation system of the nineteenth century was focused on the north east, and inhibited the growth of trading functions in New Orleans with its vast Mississippi basin hinterland as well as smaller centres such as Charleston and Savannah. The one-crop plantation economy based on slavery generated an extremely restricted appropriation of wealth, which left the great majority of the population with very low incomes. Neither the level of development of the productive forces nor the prevailing social relations of production were conducive to industrialisation even after the Civil War and the formal emancipation of the slaves. Northern capital gained increasing control of southern agriculture, creating an externally dominated and almost colonial state of underdevelopment. While some textile manufacturing moved south, the development of major growth industries in the latter part of the nineteenth century was frustrated by increasing concentration of capital in fewer and larger northern corporations.

The control exercised by major national corporations steadily increased, to become a vital feature of the *post-industrial phase* – sometimes referred to as the age of monopoly capitalism to distinguish it from the earlier more competitive phase when smaller firms predominated. This is the age of the rise of the so-called Sunbelt, which has seen the southern states in general and the south east in particular gain a disproportionately large share of economic growth. Again, what happened can be explained by the response of capital to the geography of investment laid down in the earlier phases, with new circumstances requiring new appraisals of comparative locational advantage. That the south east or old cotton-belt South should have been a major beneficiary can be attributed in part to its failure to develop substantially in the mercantile and industrial phases. While the industrial cities to the north found themselves with what had now become slow-growth sectors and an ageing urban infrastructure, the Sunbelt was not thus encumbered, and the south east had the positive advantage of low production costs, especially with respect to labour.

47

The major contributions to this contemporary phase of development are advanced electronic technology and related industries, oil and natural gas, real-estate development and tourism. Although the Sunbelt has certain natural environmental advantages in its oil and gas fields and a climate that is attractive to tourists and retirees, the extent to which today's dynamic industrial and commercial sectors have grown so effectively here owes much to the more flexible urban environments and more favourable 'business climate' when compared with the northern cities, including the status of labour. There is a lower level of unionisation and less labour militancy in the South than in the older industrial regions, and capital has responded; Peet (1983) claims that recent changes in the location of manufacturing can be explained more by the geography of class struggle than by that of climate and resources. The state has also played an important role: various federal programmes have disproportionately benefited the south east, financially assisting the construction of a modern urban infrastructure and also contributing to the growth of strategic or prestige industries associated with defence and space exploration. The relatively well-paid jobs that accompany 'high-tech' industries stimulate local demand for goods and services and hence further economic activity.

While the East South Central still has a markedly lower per capita income than other divisions, the South Atlantic now approaches the national average (Fig. 3.2). And the West South Central, including Texas, has eliminated the large gap separating it from the West North Central division at the beginning of the century. As the main focus of growth has shifted from other regions and in particular from the north east, inter-regional differences in per capita income and living standards have certainly narrowed. During the monopoly capital phase, dominated by huge corporations operating at a national scale, similar conditions of production and employment have spread to all regions. Regional economic structures have come more to resemble one another: Garnick and Friedenburg (1982) attribute half the narrowing of the gap in regional incomes from 1940 to 1979 to the more uniform

Sarasota, Florida. One of the most affluent cities in the South, with opulent homes and beach-side condominiums built during the real-estate boom associated with Sunbelt prosperity.

industrial mix. Nationally organised trade unions have also contributed to more uniform living standards through their wage bargaining. Indeed, some corporations seeking cheap labour may now be more likely to find it outside the United States, as part of their increasingly trans-national scale of operation, than in some southern pocket of poverty.

This does not mean that the pockets of poverty have disappeared, of course – far from it. It is here that the defective view of regional convergences must yield, finally, to the recognition that the current phase of development is highly selective in a geographical sense. The major metropolis is the attraction and continuing creation of the contemporary era of high-tech quasi-monopoly capital working in ever closer association with the state; the inter-metropolitan periphery is largely ignored and left to stagnate. Thus intra-regional disparities in levels of living persist and may indeed be growing, in a society increasingly polarised on the basis of participation or otherwise in modern sectors of the metropolitan economy. The trend towards equality at one spatial scale entails continuing inequality at another, as part of the same process of uneven development.

Intra-regional inequality: the case of the South

Inequality in living standards within one region may be examined briefly, to round off the argument. The region chosen is the South, broadly defined as the ten states from Arkansas and Louisiana in the west to North Carolina in the east, and from Kentucky in the north to Florida in the south. The South is not only the poorest region, despite Sunbelt growth, but also reveals some of the greatest internal disparities. This points to very low standards of living indeed in parts of the region, while elsewhere standards consistent with modern metropolitan America prevail.

Poverty is particularly severe in rural areas of the South. The situation is vividly described as follows by Deavers (1980, 353):

> While poverty causes serious human problems wherever it occurs, nowhere are there problems more severe than in rural areas where poverty is so endemic as to be reflected in areawide data on per capita or family incomes. Because of the inadequacy of local resources to support needed facilities and services, communities in these areas chronically underinvest in human resources – inadequate educational opportunities, worker training, and health care are continuing problems. For similar reasons, these areas are also short on basic community facilities and amenities that are typically found in other rural areas – poor housing, lack of public water and sewer systems, inadequate fire protection, and other such conditions are prevalent.

In addition to the intra-regional selectivity of capital investment, the South has a distinctive history and culture strongly associated with slavery and the subsequent extreme deprivation and racial discrimination experienced by its black population. Almost 40 per cent of the non-metropolitan poor in the South are black; elsewhere in America rural poverty is almost exclusively a white experience.

Table 3.3 Degree of inequality in economic and social indicators by county in the South, 1980.

Indicator	cv	Maximum	Minimum	Ratio	Fayette, Georgia	Tunica, Mississippi
Median family income ($)	19	26,939	7,171	3.76	26,939	7,685
Median value of owner-occupied housing units ($)	27	71,800	13,900	5.17	65,000	25,000
Housing with more than 1.0 persons/room (%)	44	18.3	1.4	13.07	2.1	18.3
Median school years completed	9	16.6	8.5	1.95	12.6	8.6
Infant deaths/1,000 live births	38	45.9	0	–	11.0	32.2

Note: From data for 875 counties in the states of Alabama, Arkansas, Florida, Georgia, Kentucky, Louisiana, Mississippi, North Carolina, South Carolina and Tennessee; cv is coefficient of variation.

Source: US *Census of Housing and Population*, 1980, except infant mortality which is from annual reports of State Departments of Health (average for 1979, 1980 and 1981); all courtesy of Sanford H. Bederman, Georgia State University.

Something of the degree of inequality in the South is shown in Table 3.3, based on indicators for counties making up the ten states. Data available at this scale do not always correspond with those at other scales, but some comparisons can be made with inequality by states and metropolitan areas in Table 3.2. The general impression is of higher ratios of maximum to minimum values at the county scale. The value of 0 for the lowest infant mortality makes it impossible to calculate a ratio, but the coefficient of variation shows a high degree of inequality on this indicator; existence of a maximum rate of three times that at the state scale underlines the low level of health in poor parts of the South. The contrasts within the South are highlighted by figures for the counties of Fayette, Georgia and Tunica, Mississippi, which came first and last respectively on a composite indicator for the counties of the South.

This composite indicator is mapped in Fig. 3.3, to reveal the pattern of inequality in living standards within the South. The indicator comprises the summation of standard scores on the five individual measures in Table 3.3, calculated in the manner explained in Chapter 1. There is a fairly distinct belt of low living standards extending across the map from east to west, with the highest concentration in the Yazoo district of the lower Mississippi valley. This belt corresponds with the area of highest proportions of blacks in the rural population. There is an outlier of the poverty belt in the north, in eastern Kentucky, as part of the depressed Appalachian region extending into neighbouring West Virginia. Highest living standards are associated with the metropolitan counties containing parts of major cities such as New Orleans, Birmingham, Atlanta, Columbia, Raleigh and Nashville, and along the Florida coast to include resorts like Sarasota and the prosperous communities around Cape Kennedy associated with the space exploration industry.

Fig. 3.3 Variations in living standards in the American South, 1980, based on county data for five indicators (from an original map compiled as part of a wider research project by Sanford H. Bederman, Georgia State University). *Source*: see Table 3.4.

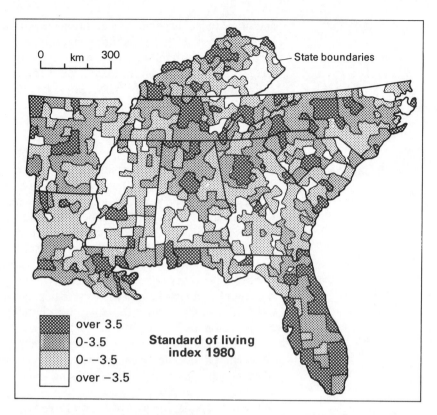

Some of the detail may be added to this broad picture of inequality in the South from a study of one state, Georgia, undertaken by Bederman and Hartshorn (1984). They identify three types of county with quite different experiences: central city, suburban and rural. The central city counties contain the inner parts of the metropolitan areas; income levels are fairly close to the state average, infant mortality somewhat higher,

Table 3.4 Degree of inequality in economic and social indicators by county in Georgia, 1950, 1970 and 1980.

Indicator	Year	Maximum	Minimum	Ratio
Median family income ($)	1950	3,868	605	6.39
	1970	12,137	3,384	3.59
	1980	26,939	9,842	2.74
Housing lacking complete	1950	66.4	16.4	4.05
plumbing (%)	1970	55.0	1.2	45.83
	1980	26.3	0.5	52.60
Median school years	1950	12.0	4.5	2.67
completed	1970	12.6	7.6	1.66
	1980	13.0	9.6	1.35
Infant deaths/1,000 live	1950	81.8	10.5	7.76
births	1970	52.9	8.0	6.61
	1980	45.9	1.7	27.00

Source: US *Census of Housing and Population*, 1950, 1970, 1980, except infant mortality which is from State of Georgia, Department of Human Resources (1950, 1970) and Department of Health (1980); data courtesy of John Offord (1950 and 1970) and Sanford H. Bederman (1980).

and housing lacking complete plumbing low, as most of the old slums have been replaced. The suburban counties have markedly higher incomes, lower infant mortality, and more spacious, well-appointed and valuable homes. The poorest rural counties stand in marked contrast, with family incomes falling below $10,000 a year, infant mortality three times the state average and up to a quarter of dwellings lacking complete plumbing.

According to the diffusionist version of the spatial organisation perspective, summarised in the previous chapter, growth impulses should spread out from the metropolis (in Georgia, Atlanta) to the periphery, as part of an equalising process. This is clearly not happening. Some metropolitan wealth is dispersed, in search of weekend homes in the Appalachian foothills and other rural areas opened up by road improvements. Rural incomes are also increased by long-distance commuting to jobs in the city. But great disparities between core and periphery remain, and in some respects they are being exacerbated. Table 3.4 provides evidence for the extent to which living standards at the county level in Georgia are converging, as revealed by figures on the extremes in 1950, 1970 and 1980 for four indicators similar to those used at the regional scale in Table 3.3. While there is a reduction in the ratio of maximum to minimum values for median family income and school years completed, the reverse is the case for housing lacking complete plumbing and infant mortality. Housing and health are improving in the worst-off counties, but they are improving faster in the well-to-do-parts of the metropolis. Inequality is therefore increasing, at this spatial scale.

Conclusion

Only brief concluding comments are required to bring this discussion back to the central theme of the relationship between social structure and spatial form. The traditional geographical preoccupation with regional resource endowment, reflecting the areal differentiation perspective, no longer has much bearing on regional inequality in living standards, as the tendency towards convergence shows. What is much more important is position in the spatial organisation or reorganisation of the economy, as capital seeks profits under changing conditions and against a changing geography of comparative advantage. But position in the sense of geographical proximity to centres of economic growth and source of wealth is not enough, as is underlined by Hancock county in Georgia with one-third of its families below the official poverty level only fifty miles or an hour's drive from Atlanta – symbol of Sunbelt prosperity. Nor is location in Atlanta itself a guarantee of high living standards, as the next chapter will show. What is crucial now is the role that particular places and their people play in the structure of a society in which benefits and burdens are subject to such unequal distribution.

4 Inequality in the American city: the case of Atlanta

Atlanta, Georgia, is in important respects a symbolic city. The epitome of the contemporary era of Sunbelt prosperity, it is also the city of *Gone with the Wind* devastated by General Sherman's 'yankee' soldiers during the American Civil War and closely bound up with the subsequent gradual resurrection of the South. It is the city where the Revd Martin Luther King lived, preached and came to prominence as leader of the black struggle for civil rights. It was the first major city in the South to elect a black mayor (Maynard Jackson in 1973). At the time of writing (1986) the mayor is another black man, Andrew Young, the country's Ambassador to the UN during the Presidency of Jimmy Carter who made human rights his special concern. Atlanta was Carter's base as he projected himself from peanut farmer and Governor of Georgia onto the national political stage, and it is here that the Presidential Library housing his papers has been built. It was also the city of Lester Maddox, who built a successful campaign for Governor on the notoriety achieved by refusing to let blacks into his restaurant at the time of integration. With these kinds of associations, inequality in Atlanta is of more than passing interest. While in some respects representative of the American city in general, Atlanta has its own special features arising from a distinctive regional setting and history, to remind us of the uniqueness that goes with locality and the actions of its people.

Atlanta is a major commercial and industrial centre. It houses the head offices of the Coca Cola Company, Southern Bell telephones, Eastern Airlines and a host of other corporations of regional and national significance. Its downtown offices, modern hotels, monorail system and new airport exude an air of prosperity associated with rapid growth. The metropolitan area of Atlanta had a population of 2.3 million in 1983 and ranked fifteenth in the nation. The City of Atlanta as a political jurisdiction comprises the central part of the metropolis, with a population of 425,000 at the time of the 1980 Census. Two-thirds of the population of the City is black, compared with a quarter in the metropolitan area as a whole. The proportion of blacks in the City has risen steadily in recent years, from 38 per cent in 1960, as white families have moved out to new suburbs beyond the City limits. The City retains some of the richest neighbourhoods in the metropolis, however, as well as substantial remnants of its poor black ghetto. While the City is, of course, an integral part of the wider metropolitan area in a simple geographical sense, the focus of this chapter is on the City of Atlanta. This is partly because of difficulties compiling data required to examine inequality beyond the City limits, and partly because the conduct of City politics is an important part of the story.

The first section of this chapter establishes the basic pattern of inequality and trends over time. Then interpretations are offered, explicitly exploring the three alternative perspectives outlined in Chapter 2 against the local background of economic, social and political change. The findings are then related to the broader theme of the mutual interdependence of spatial form and social structure, in a context that integrates this case study into the argument of the previous chapter emphasising the significance of geographical scale.

Patterns and trends

Evidence will be presented on four interrelated aspects of inequality in the City of Atlanta. The first is the pattern displayed by differences from place to place in living standards. The second is the trend over time in the degree of inequality, so as to reveal convergence or otherwise at this local scale. The third is inequality between the predominantly white and black parts of the City in aggregate, and how this has been changing. The fourth is the degree of inequality *among* predominantly white neighbourhoods as compared with those which are predominantly black, and how this has changed. The significance of these particular facets of inequality will be revealed as the argument of the chapter unfolds. All that will be said here, by way of anticipation, is that the facts fail to support a commonly espoused view of the American city becoming more equal, especially with black civil rights, economic advances and political power, but that the outcome is consistent with processes intrinsic to American capitalism.

Geographical patterns of inequality in Atlanta were first revealed by Bederman (1974; see Smith, 1977, 285–7), in a classic early study of the 'quality of life' based on eleven economic and social indicators. The pattern reflected income quite closely, and the single criterion of median family income will suffice for the present purpose. Figure 4.1 shows variation by census tracts within the City of Atlanta, for the latest date at which such figures are available. There is a clear impression of low levels around the central business district (CBD), with six tracts having less than $5,000 and a further substantial area with less than $10,000. There are three low-income outliers, the largest extending north-westwards to the City limits. Otherwise, incomes increase fairly regularly with distance from the inner-city poverty areas. The most spectacular heights are reached in the Northside suburbs where eight tracts exceed $30,000. In the southern half of the City only one tract has a median family income over $25,000. The frequency distribution diagram shows the extent of the tail in the upper-income levels, and of the spread about the tract mean.

The degree of inequality in median family income and four other conditions is indicated in Table 4.1. The ratio of maximum to minimum tract income is a massive 21.45: the median family in one Northside census tract receives more than twenty times the income of the median family in one tract near the city centre. This is ten times the ratio between the maximum and minimum state income figures, shown in Table 3.2. Median value of owner-occupied housing units in 1980 varies on a ratio of almost 15:1. The ratio for median school years completed is much smaller, reflecting a minimum determined by compulsory education and a maximum including college which cannot be exceeded.

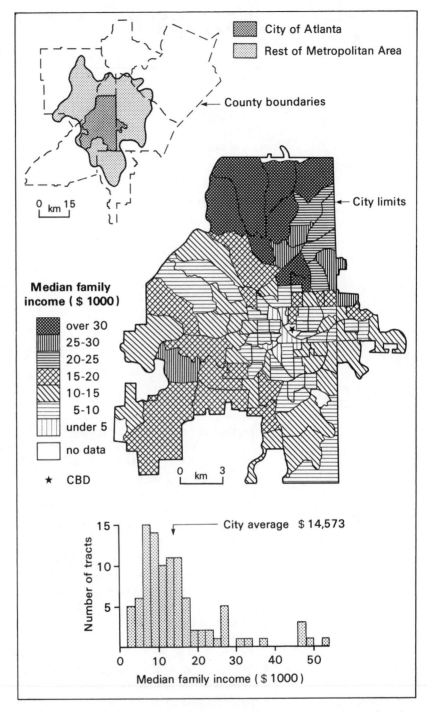

Fig. 4.1 Median family income 1979 by census tracts in the City of Atlanta, Georgia. *Source*: US *Census of Population and Housing*, 1980.

The ratio for housing with more than one person per room is rendered almost meaningless by the fact that this density is virtually non-existent in the more affluent residential areas, while zero values for some tracts make it impossible to calculate the ratio for infant mortality. A more sensitive measure of degree of inequality is provided by the coefficient of variation (explained in Chapter 1), which expresses the spread of tract values as the ratio of standard deviation to the mean. This shows four of the indicators revealing similar orders of magnitude, from about

Table 4.1 Degree of inequality in economic and social indicators by tract in Atlanta, 1960, 1970 and 1980.

Indicator	Year	Maximum	Minimum	Ratio	cv
Median family income ($)	1960	16,250	1,336	12.16	58.34
	1970	30,063	1,951	15.41	57.04
	1980	53,613	2,499	21.45	71.61
Median value of owner-	1960	25,000	5,000	5.00	43.08
occupied housing units ($)	1970	50,000	6,200	8.06	56.86
	1980	145,900	10,000	14.59	83.32
Housing with more than	1960	47.7	0.5	95.40	82.30
1.0 persons/room (%)	1970	32.4	0.2	162.00	71.73
	1980	16.7	0.1	167.00	68.32
Median school years	1960	14.7	6.2	2.37	22.58
completed	1970	16.0	7.0	2.29	19.69
	1980	16.1	7.1	2.27	19.38
Infant deaths/1,000	1960	166.7	0.0	–	74.07
live births	1970	85.7	0.0	–	60.75
	1980	52.6	0.0	–	65.49

Source: Smith (1985), Tables 2 and 6, based on data from US *Census of Housing and Population*, 1960, 1970 and 1980 and Fulton County Health Department (infant mortality figures, averages for three years).

65 for infant mortality to 83 for value of housing, with schooling subject to a much lower degree of inequality.

Turning now to trends in inequality, comparable figures for 1960 and 1970 are presented with those for 1980 in Table 4.1. For family income there is little difference in the coefficients of variation between 1960 and 1970 but a marked increase by 1980. Value of housing shows an increase from 1960 to 1970, accelerating from 1970 to 1980. The housing density indicator shows some reduction in inequality as measured by the coefficient of variation, contradicting the trend of the ratio of maximum to minimum. Median school years shows very slight falls in the coefficient, while for infant mortality inequality among tract rates fell from 1960 to 1970 but had risen by 1980. Thus the evidence can hardly sustain a convergence view of living standards at this local spatial scale; indeed, the indicators that best capture material conditions (income and value of housing) show Atlanta becoming a more unequal city during the two decades under review.

Table 4.2 provides evidence of racial inequality by residential space. For this purpose tracts have been classified as predominantly white or predominantly black by the criterion of over 90 per cent of the population belonging to the group in question. Of the 98 tracts (or combinations of tracts required to compile comparable data from one census date to another), 19 were predominantly black by this criterion in 1960 and 52 white, 33 were black in 1970 and 40 white, and in 1980 the figures were 42 black and 18 white; the shifting balance reflects the overall increase in the proportion of blacks in the City population. The impression of a highly segregated city is reinforced by the recognition that most of the black or white tracts actually have well over 90 per cent of the one race, i.e. they are almost racially exclusive *de facto* (if not,

Table 4.2   Inequality between predominantly white and black tracts in Atlanta, as shown by mean values for economic and social indicators, 1960, 1970 and 1980.

Indicator	Year	White	Black	Ratio
Median family income ($)	1960	6,380	2,396	2.66
	1970	12,146	5,710	2.13
	1980	31,612	9,473	3.34
Median value of owner-occupied housing units ($)	1960	14,763	8,942	1.65
	1970	22,705	12,124	1.87
	1980	85,272	19,939	4.28
Housing with more than 1.0 persons/room (%)	1960	6.48	33.06	5.10
	1970	4.55	19.74	4.34
	1980	0.83	8.80	10.60
Median school years completed	1960	11.66	7.94	1.47
	1970	12.25	9.54	1.28
	1980	15.41	10.69	1.44
Infant deaths/1,000 live births	1960	22.72	37.73	1.66
	1970	19.90	32.71	1.64
	1980	13.31	21.36	1.60

Note: 'Black tracts' have over 90 per cent of their population black, 'white tracts' over 90 per cent white.
Source: Smith (1985), Table 4, based on data from US *Census of Housing and Population*, 1960, 1970 and 1980 and Fulton County Health Department (infant mortality figures, averages for three years).

today, *de jure*); and in those tracts with more of a racial balance this is not usually indicative of social integration. The mean values for black and white tracts on five indicators all show the white parts of the city better off. In 1980 median family income in the predominantly white tracts was more than three times that in the black tracts and value of housing more than four times. The housing density ratio is even higher, and the measures of schooling and infant mortality both show white areas roughly one-and-a-half times as well off as the predominantly black areas.

If these figures confirm preconceptions of racial inequality, then the trends over time may come more as a surprise. After a reduction in the ratio between white and black tracts in the 1960s for median family income, the figure increased sharply during the 1970s, and the same is true of the housing density measure. There was also a substantial increase in inequality in housing value in the 1970s after only a slight increase during the earlier decade. Median school years completed became more unequal during the 1970s after a fall in the ratio during the 1960s. Only infant mortality fails to register any increase in degree of inequality as measured by the ratio of the means in the predominantly white and black tracts.

None of these figures should be construed as indicating that people in the black parts of Atlanta are worse off now in some absolute sense than ten or twenty years ago – far from it. Many blacks have achieved a substantially better standard of living, even relative to many whites. But in aggregate the black tracts are still a long way behind the predominantly white parts of the city. This can be measured in time as well as on the indicator scales: for the three conditions not affected by the changing value of money (housing density, schooling and infant mortality), the mean for the black tracts in 1980 is closely comparable to that for the white tracts in 1960.

The final question is that of degree of inequality among predominantly black and white tracts taken separately. Table 4.3 lists the coefficients of variation. These show greater inequality among black than white tracts in 1980 with respect to income and schooling but the reverse on the other indicators. However, it is the trends that are much more revealing. The figures for white tracts show inconsistent trends during the 1960s but a clear reduction in inequality on the income, housing value and education indicators during the second decade. For black tracts, all indicators except median school years completed show a steady increase in inequality over both decades.

To summarise, there is a clear pattern of low levels of living around the central part of the city, with some extensions towards the otherwise affluent outer areas. There is evidence of inequality among census tracts increasing, particularly during the 1970s. Inequality between the predominantly white and black parts of the city is increasing on certain crucial indicators, again particularly in the 1970s. And inequality among black neighbourhoods at the census tract level is increasing. These are the observations that we seek to explain, or at least make intelligible, against the background of a rapidly growing and changing metropolis. Specifically, we shall try to understand why a quarter of a century of Sunbelt prosperity has not created a more equal city, and why the ascendancy of blacks to formal political power in Atlanta in the early 1970s seems not to have been accompanied by trends in black socio-economic status which can be judged unambiguously as a welfare improvement.

Table 4.3 Degree of inequality (coefficient of variation) among predominantly white and black tracts in Atlanta, 1960, 1970 and 1980.

Indicator	Year	White	Black
Median family income ($)	1960	47.93	23.83
	1970	48.21	29.24
	1980	38.49	49.08
Median value of owner-occupied housing units ($)	1960	39.68	16.95
	1970	54.41	24.31
	1980	41.58	38.24
Housing with more than 1.0 persons/room (%)	1960	86.51	22.45
	1970	91.54	33.31
	1980	148.01	41.75
Median school years completed	1960	16.23	15.16
	1970	16.19	15.00
	1980	8.09	13.30
Infant deaths/1,000 live births	1960	105.87	26.96
	1970	82.37	38.74
	1980	103.87	48.62

Note: 'Black tracts' have over 90 per cent of their population black, 'white tracts' over 90 per cent white.

Source: Smith (1985), Table 7, based on data from US *Census of Housing and Population*, 1960, 1970 and 1980 and Fulton County Health Department (infant mortality figures, averages for three years).

Explaining inequality

In seeking to explain the various manifestations of inequality in Atlanta outlined above, we shall call directly on the three alternative perspectives of areal differentiation, spatial organisation and political economy outlined in Chapter 2. This will permit further demonstration of their respective strengths and limitations in practice, and assist the construction of an interpretation to which each perspective has a contribution to make. This procedure will fill out the local detail of the case study of Atlanta in a manner which will enable some concluding observations to be made on the underlying theme of the relationship between space and society from which patterns of inequality arise and to which these patterns contribute. The argument will of necessity be brief; more complete accounts will be found in the research on which this chapter is based (Smith, 1981, 1985).

The areal differentiation perspective holds that geographical patterns of inequality or uneven development can be accounted for by observed association with other patterns reflecting attributes of place or of the people living therein. The place attributes usually involve resources, and the association of high income or levels of living with areas of rich natural endowment carries some conviction as explanation, particularly when set in the kind of historical context related to a spatially selective process of economic development in which we attempted to understand regional inequality in the USA in the previous chapter. However, at the more local, intra-city scale a causal relationship between living standards and the resource base is quite implausible: the Northside suburbs where the rich live in Atlanta are not better endowed with natural sources of wealth than the inner city where the poor predominate. If this perspective has anything to offer in the present context, then it must be people rather than place that provides the key.

The most obvious explanation for the pattern of inequality illustrated in Fig. 4.1 is in fact the racial composition of local populations. It has already been observed that Atlanta is still a highly segregated city and that black areas are markedly worse off than those predominantly occupied by whites. This in itself should generate a spatial stratification along racial lines, as Bederman (1974) found in his study of 'quality of life' in Atlanta.

Before addressing this issue directly, some historical background to the location and status of blacks in Atlanta is required. There is a long-established black community, the population of which had already reached 60,000 by 1920. This figure grew steadily in the succeeding years, with both natural increase and migration of blacks displaced by the mechanisation of agriculture in the South. The black population was confined to a tightly prescribed ghetto around the western, eastern and southern fringes of the CBD and as still more rural poor flooded in, the extension of black residential space became inevitable. Prominent among those seeking to leave the ghetto were representations of the small 'middle-class' which had emerged within the black community. At the end of the 1940s a wedge was opened up to the west of the CBD for black residential expansion, by informal agreement with City government and the real-estate business. The scope for blacks to move into formerly white suburbs was further increased after 1960 when a

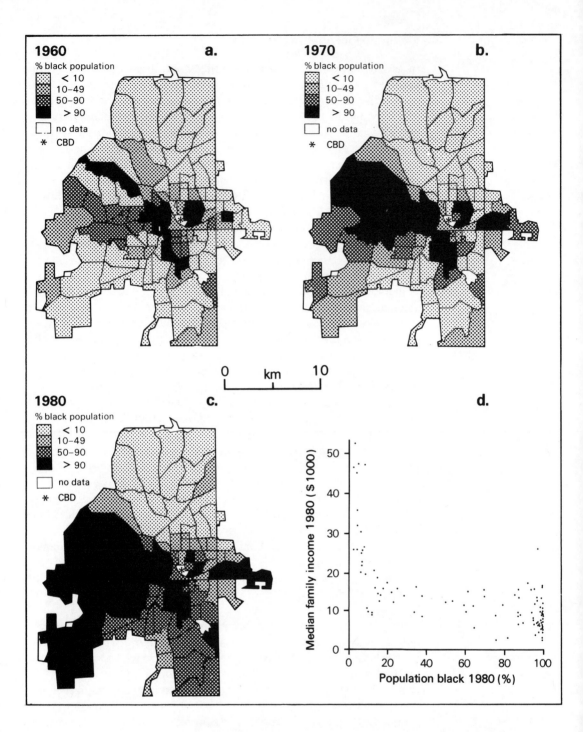

black doctor moved into a white neighbourhood to the south of the agreed wedge (a case of the crucial individual act at a crucial time); as others followed, many whites sold out and moved to new suburbs beyond the City limits, thus accelerating the pace of racial residential change. The impact of this process is illustrated in Fig. 4.2a–c, which shows the early extension of black residential space to the west of the CBD and the subsequent consolidation of black occupancy of most of the southern half of the City.

Fig. 4.2 Changes in racial composition of tract populations in Atlanta, 1960, 1970 and 1980, and relationships between racial composition and median family income, 1980. *Sources*: Smith (1985) Figs. 1 and 2; data from US *Census of Population and Housing*, 1960, 1970, 1980.

Returning to the association between living standards and race, the graph in Fig. 4.2d shows the relationship between median family income and racial composition of tract populations in 1980. The picture is not as straightforward as might have been expected. There is a clearly discernible negative relationship such that in general the higher the proportion of blacks the lower the income. Yet the form of the relationship is by no means linear. In particular, it shows a substantial spread of values among the predominantly white and predominantly black tracts. While most white tracts have high incomes, themselves subject to considerable variations, a few are quite poor. And while most black tracts have incomes below the City average, a few are better off and there is one tract in the western suburbs where median family

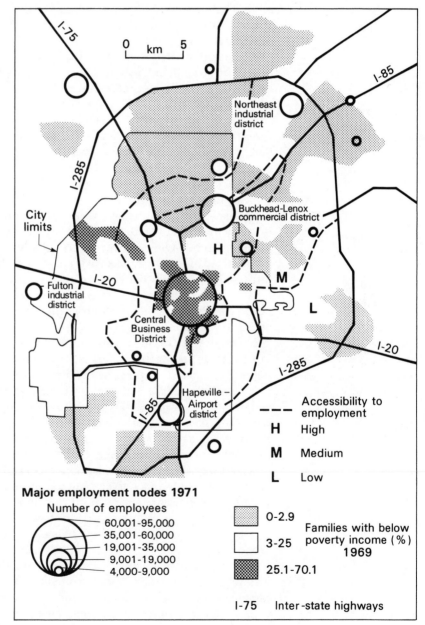

Fig. 4.3 Accessibility to employment in Atlanta, related to the incidence of families in poverty *c.* 1970. *Source*: based on Bederman and Adams (1974), Figs. 1 and 4.

61

income is exceeded only by that of the rich white Northside tracts. Thus race is significant, but only as part of a quite complex process of socio-economic spatial differentiation.

The spatial organisation perspective seeks explanation through the way in which places are interrelated, for example residences and locations of employment or other sources of need satisfaction. The concentration of poverty in the inner parts of the cities in the USA is sometimes attributed to difficulty of access to increasingly dispersed job opportunities. Decentralisation of industrial and commercial activities has been a major feature of the spatial reorganisation of the American metropolis in recent years and Atlanta is no exception; as elsewhere, limited public transport and lack of a car reliable enough for regular freeway driving place the inner-city poor at a disadvantage. Even Atlanta's new monorail system is designed largely to get suburban commuters in to the CBD rather than to facilitate movement in the other direction.

An attempt by Bederman and Adams (1974) to see how far inner city poverty in Atlanta in 1970 could be attributed to problems of access to employment is still relevant today. Figure 4.3 shows the major centres of employment in and around the metropolis, along with the areas in which more than a quarter of families had incomes below the official poverty level. The least poverty-stricken areas are also shown, to highlight the suburban affluence belt. Superimposed on this are contours of a surface calculated by Bederman and Adams to summarise the level of accessibility of residents to jobs in five centres representative of the overall distribution of employment (Fulton, Buckhead-Lenox, Northeast, Hapeville-Airport and CBD). The result is, on the face of it, counterintuitive: the inner-city poverty areas are within the zone of *highest* overall accessibility. This is not only because a central location is best placed with respect to the aggregate of dispersed job centres, but also because the CBD still contains the largest localised concentration of employment. Thus, whatever is keeping inner-city residents disproportionately poor, it is not physical access to work.

For more penetrating insight into the processes generating inequality in Atlanta, including its racial manifestations, we may now turn to the political-economy perspective. This must be broad enough to encompass the activities of city government as well as the kind of social and economic considerations which have already arisen in exploring aspects of the areal differentiation and spatial organisation perspective. And it must have sufficient reference to the time dimension to make some sense of our earlier observations concerning trends in inequality.

A starting point is provided by Bederman and Adams (1974). While accessibility to jobs failed to account for the geographical distribution of poverty or 'underemployment', and percentage of blacks in the population provided only a moderate statistical explanation, they found high negative correlations with median school years completed, proportion of labour force in service-related jobs and proportion of families with a female head. These observations highlight certain crucial features of the operation of the market for labour which, under capitalism, determines who works and for what reward. Those with limited education and skills can generate little by way of value of goods and services and hence little if any profit for employers; they will thus earn low wages, if in work at all. The best to which many can aspire is menial service-sector employment, which is often irregular and subject to the vagaries of hotel, conference and restaurant trade which itself reflects the prosperity of the wider economy. Female (often black) heads of families are in a particularly disadvantaged position, less able to conform to regular hours of employment than the conventional male 'breadwinner' with wife at home looking after the children. As Bederman and Adams (1974, 385) observed: 'Atlanta's critically underemployed are mainly black female heads of families, and no matter where they live in the metropolis they have neither the skills to qualify them for the new jobs being created, nor the opportunity to acquire marketable skills'. And with low incomes goes poor housing, poor local schools, inability to afford fee-for-service health care, and high vulnerability to crime that accompanies residence in a poor neighbourhood. For those who do have the skills and enterprise that the market rewards more generously, Atlanta offers a life of great material comfort and some sophistication, with the prospect of sumptuous Northside homes and prestigious country clubs as spurs to further achievement.

Now the markets which allocate such conspicuous differences in living standards are not universal mechanisms operating independent of place or time. They are products of a particular form of human society, in which the private profit imperative drives economic activity and excludes those unable to generate the value of the cost of hiring them. In the USA the intrinsically competitive character of capitalism is heightened by a culture and ideology that encourages individual pursuit of material success to the point of extreme virtue, and attributes poverty largely to the personal failings of the poor. Far from being a problem, the poor can be a convenient source of cheap labour available as and when required, and maintained by programmes of support well short of the welfare state provisions that are taken for granted in most of Western Europe.

A concentration of inner-city poverty can become a problem (for those other than the poor), however, if it threatens important elements of social reproduction. Such a threat need not take the dramatic form of urban riots, referred to in Chapter 1; to prejudice profit-making or the value of capital accumulation in the form of investments may be sufficient to precipitate action. This happened in a number of American cities in the 1950s and 1960s, including Atlanta. The specific problem was the threat to continued viability of a CBD virtually surrounded by poor black neighbourhoods, at a time when the outward expansion of the metropolis was in any event encouraging the decentralisation of downtown business. A brief review of the conduct of the urban renewal programme in Atlanta extends the application of the perspective of political economy to incorporate city government and the planning process.

While urban renewal is usually dignified as slum clearance, to the benefit of those living in unsalubrious environments, its more fundamental purpose was to facilitate a spatial restructuring required to maintain the viability of the CBD. Commonly seen as a euphemism for 'negro removal', urban renewal in Atlanta was responsible for the clearance of extensive areas of poor, largely black-occupied housing adjoining the city centre. Hartshorn *et al.* (1976, 44) reported almost 67,000 people displaced by some form of local government activity during the urban renewal era from 1957 to 1967, involving a loss of 21,000 housing units, while only 5,000 new units of public housing were constructed. This result was achieved by using freeways and other civic construction projects so positioned as to eliminate large areas of poor neighbourhoods. In a detailed examination of the programme, Stone (1976, 177–8) is clear as to the basic motives:

> One of the main objectives of the city's renewal effort has been the creation of buffers between the city's commercial core and low-income residential areas. Thus the major thrust of the city's urban renewal program was not to provide land for commercial redevelopment . . . Rather it was, especially in the 1960s, a policy of building 'support' facilities – the stadium and the civic centre – which could have been located elsewhere with less residential dislocation but which in that event would not have served as buffers between low-income citizens and CBD commercial activity.

What new commercial development did take place was within the existing CBD behind its cordon sanitaire; the dramatic new hotels and office blocks of Atlanta's downtown skyline today are illustrative of the 'success' of urban renewal. Of those inner-city residents displaced, only about one-third were rehoused by the City, the rest filtering out to the next zone of low-rental housing, thus accelerating its deterioration. Poverty areas were eliminated but the poor were not: they were simply relocated.

The implementation of a decade of large-scale urban renewal required a major commitment on the part of the City government, to a programme which generated a conspicuously unequal distribution of costs and benefits. Stone (1976) observed what he termed 'system bias' in the consistency with which the Atlanta City government favoured some particular policy and hence that section of the population standing to gain from it. It was not simply a case of 'businessmen' influencing 'politicians': the two were closely synonymous in Atlanta's power structure, at least up to the late 1960s. Nor was it a case of a

Downtown Atlanta, with Interstate 75 in the foreground. The Interstate highway forms part of the buffer zone between the CBD and inner-city poverty areas created by 'urban renewal'.

homogenous business class running the city to their own common purpose: there were conflicts between big and small businesses, for example, the latter resenting tax increases to fund projects which they saw as largely benefiting the former. But sufficient consensus was achieved to drive the programme through: 'the business community was able to exert a strong and unified influence on the renewal process, while blacks were unable to make anything more than fragmented and short-lived efforts to shape renewal policy' (Stone, 1976, 81). That some black neighbourhoods were eventually able to mobilise opposition could be attributed in part to a growing cohesion initially forged in the civil rights struggle. Non-affluent whites, it appears, had no voice in the process at all.

Such were the power alignments in Atlanta as urban renewal came to an end in the latter part of the 1960s. But the city was soon to see a major political change which might have been expected radically to alter the course of its development. In 1973 a black lawyer, Maynard Jackson, was elected mayor, by an alliance between the growing black population and 'liberal' whites who viewed the traditional Southern attitudes of racial supremacy associated with some earlier white mayors as inconsistent with Atlanta's new status as centre of Sunbelt prosperity. However, the expectation that the poor (largely black) population of the City might now gain disproportionately, at the expense of Atlanta's customary (largely white) beneficiaries of economic growth, was not to be fulfilled. Indeed, the separation of political power from economic power, manifest in the election of Jackson and a City Council which was half black, represented a major structural break with the past: the cohesion between City Hall and business which had made the urban renewal programme possible had lost its common identity and purpose.

The scope of the Jackson mayoralty to benefit significantly the inhabitants of the poor (black) parts of the city was thus limited. Greater neighbourhood stability was achieved along with some rehabilitation, as a result of urban planning more sensitive to local needs than were the massive renewal projects. Blacks benefited from the redistribution of City jobs, most notably in the Police Department which had a practical as well as symbolic importance to ghetto residents accustomed to what they saw as harassment by white officers. City construction projects provided further means of advancing blacks, through contract requirements relating to black employment. However, the overall impact of these measures was not very great. And those who bore the costs were not the white business owners but low- to middle-income whites – the same group who saw their neighbourhoods infiltrated or taken over by blacks displaced through urban renewal or moving into the western and southern suburbs. The main black beneficiaries of the Jackson mayoralty were, arguably, the black business and professional 'middle class', from whom Jackson himself was recruited, and whose interests, aspirations and life styles are increasingly congruent with those of the white business community. Burman (1979) sees a growing cleavage between the black bourgeoisie and the mass of Atlanta's blacks, the economic advance of the black middle class leaving the rest of the black population probably worse off relative to the whole of American society than it had been ten years earlier.

This outline of recent political developments, along with other elements in the political-economy perspective, may now be brought to bear on the specific issues of inequality for which we seek an interpretation. Figure 4.4 provides a graphic summary of the differential experience of the predominantly white and black parts of the City from 1960 through 1970 and on to 1980, as indicated by the changing distribution of median family income. The income figures have been transformed into standard scores (see Chapter 1) for comparability: thus the mean for all tracts each year is 0 and the standard deviation is 1. In 1960 there were a substantial number of white tracts ranged about the mean; these had been reduced by 1970 and had virtually disappeared by 1980 as the inhabitants of these areas had become better off in a relative as well as absolute sense or left the City for suburbs beyond to be replaced by blacks. The trend for predominantly black tracts is a broadening of the distribution, from its narrow concentration at the bottom of the scale in 1960 to more dispersal (inequality) in 1970 and 1980. The continuing inequality between white and black parts of Atlanta is illustrated by the almost complete lack of coincidence between the two income distributions in 1980. Some blacks are clearly better off than they were, relatively as well as absolutely, but so are many whites. And the black inner-city

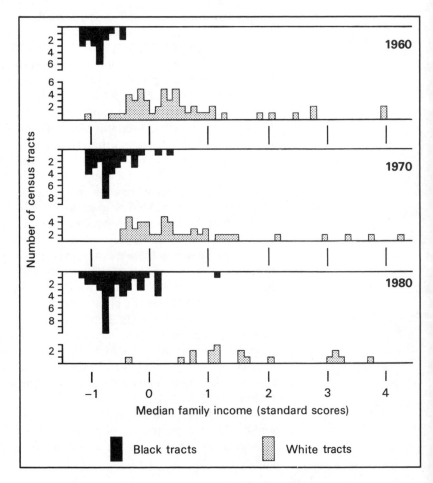

Fig. 4.4 The changing distribution of census tracts in Atlanta with more than 90 per cent whites or blacks, by median family income. *Source*: US *Census of Population and Housing*, 1960, 1970, 1980.

poor remain so, anchoring the bottom end of the income distribution at a level well below that of the poorest white tract. It is thus that Atlanta has become a more unequal city, spatially and racially.

Conclusion

The previous chapter offered an interpretation of regional inequality in the United States in which the convergence tendency arising from the spread of similar kinds of economic activity and conditions of production throughout the land was continually disturbed by the geographical selectivity of capital as it moves around a surface of differentiated opportunities for profit. Atlanta is one of the cities selected by this process for rapid growth and rising aggregate prosperity. That the City, and its wider metropolis, was able to realise its potential in changing circumstances was due in no small measure to the fact that, as Perry and Watkins (1977, 41) say of the Sunbelt cities in general, it was 'in a more flexible position to shift with the changing needs of the economy'. This flexibility involved both spatial form and social structure, functioning together under the guidance but by no means total control of the major local institutions of economic and political power.

The spatial form inherited from the past was in some senses helpful but in some an encumbrance. Atlanta was a focal point of regional transportation, had an established business district with no serious constraints on its expansion, ample land around the fringe for new industrial, commercial and residential development, and few of the physical inconveniences of outmoded industrial quarters from an earlier era. But the past had generated one major problem, in the shape of a

Left:
Black Atlanta: remnants of the inner-city ghetto in Mechanicsville which survived urban renewal (top); upper-income housing in Cascade Heights in the western suburbs, transferred from white to black occupancy in the late 1960s and early 1970s (bottom).

Right:
White Atlanta: Cabbage-town – a poor inner-city neighbourhood, built for workers of a nearby textile mill and later occupied predominantly by migrants from Appalachia (top); Buckhead, the height of white affluence in Atlanta's Northside suburbs, still almost exclusively occupied by whites (bottom).

poor inner-city black population swelled by migrants from the countryside; the ghetto frustrated the aspirations of upwardly mobile blacks, and threatened the existing viability of the CBD and its future growth potential. The effectiveness with which the City's power structure organised the selective expansion of black residential space without threatening Northside exclusivity, and secured the CBD via urban renewal, is indicative of the importance of creating a spatial form consistent with the new needs. This process included the modernisation of the transportation infrastructure, with freeways constructed or widened and a rapid transit system created with almost total disregard for the inherited built form. The changes in social structure which have accompanied spatial reorganisation have permitted the selective advancement of blacks while avoiding both the serious racial tensions and the radical politics which might otherwise have discouraged the external (national, rather than regional and local) capital which has become increasingly involved in Atlanta's growth. The necessary and perhaps sufficient conditions for Sunbelt prosperity were thus achieved.

Just as this restructuring responded to an inherited pattern of inequality, so the outcome has brought further change. The basic pattern of inner-city poverty and suburban affluence survives, subject to rearrangement of detail as a result of urban renewal and the further displacement of some of the poor with the gentrification of a few inner neighbourhoods of deteriorated 'Victorian' mansions. But its racial undertones have become significantly blurred, with the selective upward (and outward) mobility of blacks joining an increasingly trans-racial bourgeoisie and capitalist class. The former race-space polarisation is thus being replaced by one in which class is the salient criterion. The well-do-do of each race still live in largely segregated neighbourhoods, but they increasingly share similar standards of living differentiated even more sharply from the residual black ghetto population and the pockets of poor whites. Between the extremes, black advances have been more than matched by those of the whites, but as an outcome of unequal economic opportunity rather than of overt racial discrimination; it is personal attributes as evaluated by market mechanisms (albeit imperfectly) that largely allocate life chances, not race or even location at the scale of the city.

Barely six miles or as many minutes' freeway driving separate the inner-city poverty areas of Cabbagetown (white) and Mechanicsville (black) from the suburban affluence of Cascade Heights (black) and Buckhead (white). Such places represent the extremes of inequality in Atlanta. Yet their quality of life arises only in a trivial sense from place itself: what matters far more is their position in the interdependent structures of spatial and social relations, formed and reformed in the distinctive local response to the imperatives of the wider economy. That a process of spatial and social change as volatile as that observed in Atlanta should have been accomplished in such an apparently orderly manner cannot, finally, be explained without reference to the role of individuality as well as of locality. This was the city of people who could compromise as well as compete, of the conciliator as well as the assertive; of men like Martin Luther King as well as Lester Maddox.

5   Inequality under socialism: the case of the USSR

Socialism raises egalitarian expectations. While capitalism is intrinsically competitive and by its very nature generates and perpetuates inequality, socialism should involve a harmonious form of society directed explicitly towards the reduction of inequality if not its complete elimination. That socialism in practice can reveal quite a considerable degree of inequality – personally and geographically – is indicative of the actual impossibility of creating an equal world. It also raises the question of what form such inequality takes, as an expression of the particular kind of society that we term socialism.

It is important at the outset to make a distinction between socialism and communism. The term 'communist', like Marxist, tends to be used indiscriminately in countries like Britain and the USA, to describe anything (or anybody) not affiliated with capitalism, which is itself taken to be synonymous with democracy and even freedom. Strictly speaking, however, communism is an ideal form of society which Karl Marx envisaged as the ultimate achievement of a process of change initiated by the overthrow of capitalism. A communist society is supposed to be classless, based on the common ownership of property, and without the necessity for a state; it operates according to Marx's maxim: from each according to ability, to each according to need. Such a society does not exist, though there are some described as communist by the criterion of being governed by a Communist Party dedicated (at least nominally) to the pursuit of communism.

Socialism is a form of society which historically may come between capitalism and communism. It is characterised by public or state ownership of the means of production and central planning of economic and related activity. The crucial difference when compared with communism is that under socialism, income – along with some goods and services – is distributed not strictly according to need but as reward for quantity and quality of work performed. The term 'socialist' should not be applied to a so-called mixed economy (i.e. capitalist but with a state-run sector), or for example to Britain under a Labour government, for the prevailing social relations remain capitalist even though there may be some state ownership of the means of production and a policy commitment to reducing inequality.

Like capitalism, socialism can take a variety of forms. There can be different social formations, reflecting its pre-existing capitalist or feudal mode of production, its history and culture, and also its geography. The case of the Soviet Union has been chosen to explore and to some extent exemplify patterns of inequality under socialism, recognising that it has its own unique features as well as similarities with the socialism practised elsewhere in Eastern Europe and some countries in other parts of the world. The objective of this case study is as before: to attempt to understand inequality and its geographical expression as a reflection of the mutual interdependence of social structure and spatial form. Comparison with the case of the USA will highlight the relationship between specific and quite different political, economic and social conditions and their particular manifestations in inequality. The focus is largely on the one city of Moscow, but a review of regional inequality is provided by way of background. First, though, a little more about socialism and how it differs from capitalism.

The nature of socialism

The discussion of alternative explanatory perspectives in Chapter 2 concluded with a very general view of human activity as a process of social developments (Fig. 2.3). The underlying concept was that of social reproduction, whereby a particular form of society is perpetuated, or changed in some quantitative or qualitative respect, i.e. by expanded productive output or the resolution of problems frustrating further development along the same trajectory. The advent of socialism may be construed as a change brought about by the action of individuals and groups responding to the inability of an existing social structure to function in a manner consistent with its continuing reproduction. Thus a set of social relations and political institutions may exist which eventually becomes incapable of promoting the kind of economic development required to satisfy the basic consumption needs of the mass of the people, and if orderly change proves impossible revolution can take place. This was the case in Russia in 1917.

Fig. 5.1 An outline of the process of social development under socialism.

The concept of social reproduction provides a framework for an initial examination of the nature of socialism. Figure 5.1 is a specific version of Fig. 2.3 which captures the basic features of the development of a socialist society. On the left is simple reproduction whereby there is just enough material production to renew labour via consumption and

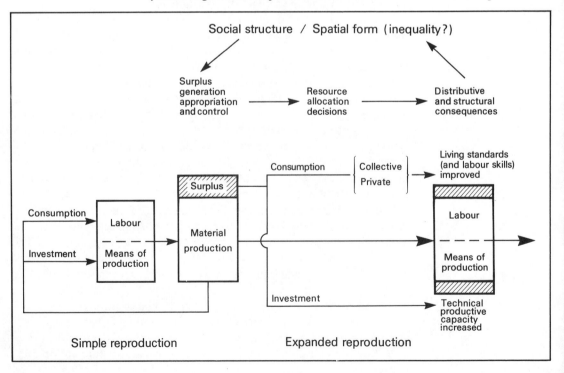

70

the means of production via investment (along with the state and other institutions, not shown here). The generation of a surplus enables expanded reproduction to take place. While under capitalism the surplus is appropriated by the capitalist and landowning class to dispose of in their own interests, under socialism it is acquired by the state on behalf of the population at large. This is possible because the means of production are not in the private ownership which legitimises private appropriation of the surplus, and permits the central determination of how it is to be used in the general interest.

The right-hand part of the diagram shows how the disposal of the surplus takes place in expanded reproduction. Central decisions determine the allocation of resources between investment (in particular sectors and places) to increase the technical capacity to produce more goods and services, and consumption to enhance people's living standards and also their productivity (through improved education, training, health care and so on). Although some consumption is private, in the form of goods and certain personal services acquired through the expenditure of income, much is provided collectively. The scope of collective consumption distinguishes socialism from capitalism, for the services provided by the state, including most retailing, leisure and cultural facilities, are much more comprehensive than offered by the 'welfare state' under Western European capitalism. The balance between collective and private consumption is a crucial decision, not least because of the difference in attitudes associated with the co-operative element in collective consumption compared with the more self-serving character of private consumption which depends on how much income can be earned.

The upper part of the diagram relates the process of reproduction to our broader concerns. The allocation of the surplus will have certain distributive consequences, in the sense that some people in some places will gain in relation to others elsewhere. For example, the decision to invest on a large scale to enhance the productive output of certain regions may raise living standards there. An example is Siberia, where economic development is being promoted for strategic reasons as well as to utilise the vast natural resources and where labour recruitment is encouraged by relatively high living standards via generous wages and collective consumption provision. Resources can be directed towards underdeveloped or poor regions so as to reduce inequality, in a manner which is impossible under capitalism. The prevailing distributive rule – to each according to work performed – will, however, advantage people (and places) responsible for work on which society places high value, and this can generate a new kind of inequality. Thus socialist planning will result in a particular spatial form arising from uneven development inherited from the past and changed according to central government objectives in which the need efficiently to produce the goods on which (expanded) reproduction depends will at times and perhaps quite frequently transcend the goal of reducing inequality. This emerging spatial form will have implications for social structure, and this will feed back to reinforce or perhaps change the manner in which the next round of surplus is generated, appropriated and distributed.

The particular nature of Soviet-style socialism is the subject of varied interpretations (see, for example, Lane, 1978, Chapter 6). In seeking our own understanding of this particular society through the case material that follows, the only further guidance to be offered at this stage is in the form of some structural features which may be summarised as a series of contradictions between equalitarian expectations and social reality. Equality among regions and between city and countryside is a state objective, yet the uneven resource base and geography inherited from Tsarist times must influence the development process. Redistribution in pursuit of greater equality necessitates a surplus, yet its efficient production may require the further development of already prosperous regions. Equalisation calls for central co-ordination, yet this itself may generate inequalities between centre and periphery. Control of surplus production is required for its disposal in pursuit of what is taken to be the general interest, yet this carries with it the possibility of those who exercise control becoming an elite who advantage themselves. The great personal inequalities in income and wealth under capitalism are eliminated under socialism, yet differential rewards acting as incentives still make some people better off than others. Large-scale ownership of property cannot be inherited, yet as long as the family remains the basic unit of social life other advantages can be transmitted from one generation to another. Finally, the creation of an equalitarian society requires a collectivist outlook by the people (sometimes dignified as the creation of a 'new communist man'), yet some features of contemporary life as well as the bourgeois past preserve and perhaps extend the realm of individualistic behaviour. Resolving tensions generated by such contradictions is an important part of the dynamics of Soviet socialist society.

Regional inequality

This section presents such evidence as is available, from the latest published Soviet data, as to the pattern and extent of inequality and whatever tendency towards regional convergence may be observed. Paucity of information constrains the examination of inequality in the Soviet Union. There are no figures published for per capita income, though estimates can be compiled with some difficulty, and the Soviet authorities are not inclined to disseminate data on the kind of economic and social condition used as indicators of living standards in earlier chapters of this book. The official statistical yearbook of the USSR (*Narodnoye Khoziaistvo*) does, however, contain figures on a few relevant variables which are sufficient for the present purpose.

The value of retail trade per inhabitant provides a reasonable indication of purchasing power. The most obvious geographical scale at which to examine regional inequality is that of the fifteen Soviet Socialist Republics which comprise the Soviet Union. As these are more or less synonymous with different nationalities within the large and diverse territory forged into a single nation state mostly before the 1917 revolution, and as reducing inequality among nationalities has been an explicit Soviet aim, this scale has a special significance. Figures for 1984 for retail sales from state and co-operative trading (which accounts for most retailing in the USSR) show a range from 1,681 roubles per capita in Estonia to 679 in Azerbaijan, a ratio of 2.59:1.

However, the republic scale is inconvenient in one important respect.

Fig. 5.2 Retail sales per capita in the USSR, by republics and regions of the RSFSR, and by subdivisions of RSFSR in relation to urbanisation. *Source*: *Narodnoye Khoziaistvo SSSR*, 1984 and *Narodnoye Khoziaistvo RSFSR*, 1984.

The Russian Soviet Federal Socialist Republic (RSFSR) covers about three-quarters of the country and accounts for half its population. To examine patterns of inequality at anything other than a very general level thus requires the breakdown of the RSFSR. This can be done by taking the ten economic planning regions into which the Russian Republic is customarily divided. Figure 5.2a maps retail sales per capita by republics and within the RSFSR by regions, using proportions of the figure for the whole of the USSR to highlight the pattern. A clear picture of regional distinction is revealed, with the highest figure in the

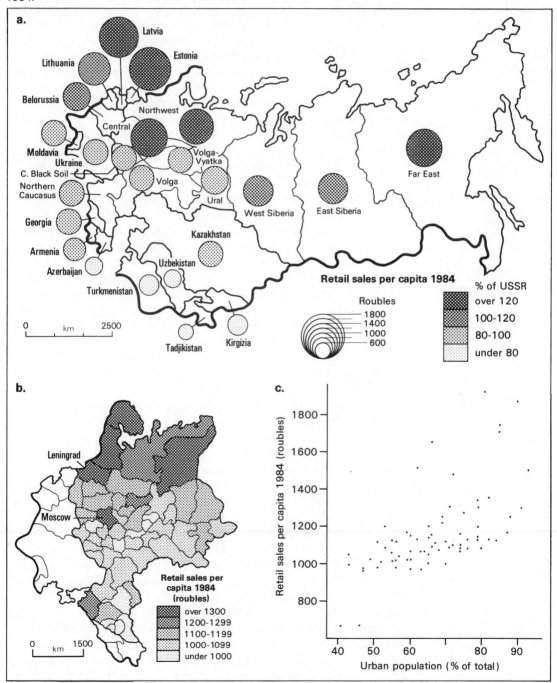

Baltic republics of Estonia, Latvia and Lithuania, in the Central and Northwest regions of the RSFSR (containing the cities of Moscow and Leningrad respectively), and in the Far East. The lowest levels are in the Asiatic republics of Kirgizia, Tadjikistan, Uzbekistan and Turkmenistan and in Azerbaijan. Intermediate values are recorded in Kazakhstan, the two trans-Caucasian republics of Georgia and Armenia, and in the belt from the European republics of Belorussia, the Ukraine and Moldavia across to the Ural region.

Proceeding to a finer spatial scale is made possible by data for over seventy subdivisions of the RSFSR, known as *oblasts*, along with some other territories usually defined for local nationality groups. *Oblast* figures for retail sales are subject to greater inequality than by republics; they range from 1,921 roubles per capita in 1984 in Magadan (in the north-eastern corner of the Far East region) to 669 in the Dagestan Autonomous Soviet Socialist Republic in the Caucasus. The ratio is 2.87:1. The pattern of variation at the *oblast* scale in the European part of the RSFSR is shown in Fig. 5.2b. A north-to-south decrease in retail sales per capita is revealed, but with some interesting local detail including a band of *oblasts* with less than 1,000 roubles to the south-east of Moscow. Apart from Moscow, and beyond the area shown in the map, the highest retail sales per capita are found in the Far East where places like Kamchatka, Sakhalin, Yakutsk and Magadan have figures exceeding 1,600 owing to high wages (and living costs). Some of the high values in the north in Fig. 5.2b also reflect the tendency for positive discrimination in favour of people in remote or harsh environments.

Figure 5.2c shows the relationship between retail sales per capita within the RSFSR and the proportion of the population that is urban. The tendency for living standards by this criterion to increase with urbanisation is fairly clear, even in Siberia or the Far East, the figures for which refer largely to urban centres created or enlarged as part of the strategy of economic development.

Urbanisation is an important dimension of inequality in the USSR. About 100 million people live in cities with over 100,000 inhabitants and there are more than twenty cities of over 1 million. The superiority of city life is widely recognised; as Morton and Stuart (1984, 5) put it, 'In the eyes of most Soviet citizens, cities are the most, indeed the only, desirable places to live, and the larger the city the better – ideally Moscow or the capitals of republics'. The level of living in cities tends to reflect not only size and status within the national control hierarchy but also geographical location so that cities in relatively rich republics will be better off than those in Soviet central Asia, for example. Deviations from this pattern will be largely an outcome of occupational composition of the population, with high living standards in cities specialising in such activities as mining which are highly paid. But the sharpest contrasts are between city and countryside. The rural areas of the USSR suffer from remoteness and from the preponderance of agriculture which is relatively poorly paid.

It is an explicit objective of Soviet planning to reduce inequality in living standards from place to place. Progress in narrowing the gap between city and countryside or among cities is hard to judge from the available data, but changes in both degree and pattern of inequality at the scale of the republics can be examined with some precision. The use of retail sales is complicated by shifts in the value of the rouble as well as other difficulties, so we shall adopt alternative indicators. Table 5.1 shows changes in the number of doctors per 100,000 inhabitants from 1940 to 1984. The Soviets inherited a highly unequal distribution of health services, with a ratio of 45:1 between the highest and lowest republics for doctors in relation to population in 1913. By 1940 this had been reduced to 3.5:1 and further reductions are recorded up to the latest data available, by this measure of degree of inequality and also by the mean percentage deviation from the national average. However, the pattern of inequality has not changed very much. This is highlighted by the republic figures expressed as percentages of that for the USSR, which show the Baltic republics along with Georgia consistently above average (i.e. over 100) and the Asiatic republics consistently below. Thus the process of regional convergence has not generated a substantially different geography of advantage.

Table 5.2 summarises republic change in another condition related to health services. The ratio of highest to lowest hospital beds per capita in 1913 was 65.5:1; now it is less than 2:1. Again, the geographical pattern has changed little, closely resembling that for doctors. The figures show a slight increase in degree of inequality from 1970 to 1984, and a similar result appears in figures for students in higher education per 1,000 inhabitants. Figures for living space per capita in urban housing (an important indicator of living standards in a country with a perpetual housing shortage) show little change in degree of inequality among republics over the past four decades and also little change in the familiar pattern of highest levels in the Baltic and some other European republics and lowest levels in Soviet central Asia.

Table 5.1   Doctors per 100,000 inhabitants by republics of the USSR, 1940–84.

	1940		1960		1970		1984	
	No.	% of USSR	No.	% of USSR	No.	% of USSR	No.	% of USSR
RSFSR	82	109	208	104	290	106	441	107
Estonia	100	127	239	120	331	121	455	110
Latvia	132	167	264	132	359	131	480	117
Lithuania	67	82	174	87	275	100	424	103
Belorussia	57	72	164	82	258	94	367	89
Ukraine	84	106	199	100	277	101	405	98
Moldavia	42	53	143	72	205	75	363	88
Georgia	133	168	330	165	364	133	525	127
Armenia	75	95	240	120	287	105	371	90
Azerbaijan	100	127	237	119	250	91	369	90
Kazakhstan	43	54	140	70	218	80	363	88
Turkmenistan	76	96	187	94	213	78	311	75
Uzbekistan	47	59	139	70	201	73	327	79
Tadjikistan	41	52	127	64	159	58	260	63
Kirgizia	38	48	154	76	208	76	324	79
USSR	79		200		274		412	
Ratio max.:min.	3.50		2.60		2.29		2.02	
Mean % deviation		32.9		23.1		18.1		15.0

Source: Narodnoye Khoziaistvo SSSR, 1984.

Table 5.2   Inequality in hospital beds per 10,000 inhabitants by republics of the USSR, 1940–84.

	1940	1960	1970	1984
USSR	40	80	109	129
Republic maximum	63	107	119	139
Republic minimum	24	67	92	83
Ratio max.:min.	2.63	1.60	1.29	1.67
Mean % deviation	20.5	7.80	7.93	10.6

Source: Narodnoye Khoziaistvo SSSR, 1984.

Finally, Table 5.3 shows trends in the degree of inequality in distribution of doctors among subdivisions of the RSFSR. Figures for the cities of Moscow and Leningrad are included to highlight their advantage over other areas. Inequality has been reduced substantially and consistently from 1940 to 1984, especially when Moscow is included. If the city and surrounding *oblast* are taken together, the figure in 1984 is 74.2 compared with 62.3 in the highest other *oblast*; in 1940 the figures for the same areas were 23.4 and 13.3 respectively.

Table 5.3   Inequality of doctors per 100,000 inhabitants within the RSFSR, 1940–84.

	1940	1960	1970	1984
Moscow	41.7	59.1	74.1	103.2
Leningrad	32.8	59.6	70.0	85.3
Oblast maximum	13.3	34.6	45.7	62.3
Oblast minimum	2.0	8.8	15.7	27.6
Ratio max.:min.	6.65	3.93	2.91	2.26
Ratio Moscow:min.	20.85	6.72	4.72	3.74

Source: Narodnoye Khoziaistvo RSFSR, 1984.

The evidence assembled here is broadly consistent with other research on regional inequality in the USSR (e.g. Nechemias, 1980; Schiffer, 1985). The early post-war period showed convergence of living standards at the scale of republics and economic regions, with an evening-off and a slight increase in degree of inequality of some conditions in more recent years. A ratio of about 2:1 between highest and lowest levels is found on most conditions, with the best-off and worst-off parts of the country tending to be the same as before. At the *oblast* scale, within the RSFSR, the evidence points more convincingly to a continuing reduction in equality (see also Cole and Harrison, 1978), but it does not follow that city and countryside disparities are being reduced for it may just be that the (increasingly) urban populations of *oblasts* are becoming more equal but with a continuing gap between them and those on the farms.

These observations may now be related, briefly, to the outline of the structure of socialist society in the previous section. The degree of inequality inherited from the pre-Soviet period was akin to that between a relatively advanced industrial nation and poor parts of the Third World (i.e. the Asiatic republics). To generate the surplus product required to promote more even development has necessitated the further growth of the already relatively advanced parts of European USSR along with resource-rich virgin territories like Siberia which were not poor but undeveloped. The difficulty of pulling the Asiatic republics up to a level of living comparable with the national average has been compounded by rapid rates of population growth related to cultural traditions different from those in the European republics. There has nevertheless been a striking reduction in degree of inequality among republics and also more locally. This has been accomplished by industrialisation (and the associated process of urbanisation), which has transferred many people in hitherto underdeveloped regions from agriculture to better-paid occupations, and by the progress made towards evening-out social service provision (e.g. in health care) through planned growth of collective consumption. Those inequalities which still exist arise not from the differentiated profit surface as sequentially appraised and restructured by private business under capitalism, but from the continuing necessity for the state to be regionally selective in its investment strategy in pursuit of productive efficiency (which is elusive without the discipline of competitive markets), from the difficulty of providing services and the personnel to run them in the remote and (to urban-trained professionals) uninviting countryside, and from the perpetual and perhaps increasing attraction, relative prosperity and occasional excitement of the major city. It is to the Soviet Union's largest city that we now turn, for what further insight it can yield on inequality and its significance under socialism.

Inequality in the Soviet city: the case of Moscow

With a population of 8,462,000 at the beginning of 1985, Moscow is the largest city in the USSR and almost twice the size of the second city of Leningrad. As capital of the Soviet Union as well as of the RSFSR it has a special significance in national life. The presence of the Bolshoi along with the Kremlin underlines the city's cultural as well as political pre-eminence. And as the city most frequently visited by foreign tourists, it has been deliberately fostered as a showplace of Soviet socialism, most notably through the facelift undertaken before the 1980 Olympic Games. While representative of certain general features of Soviet urban life and social dynamics, Moscow can hardly be described as typical, if only because of its size and planned superiority. But it is the cities at the forefront of a society's development, like Atlanta in the American Sunbelt, that most vividly reveal the contradictions worked out in the process of change; so it may be with Moscow.

To live anywhere within Moscow may be considered a privilege for a Soviet citizen. Access to Moscow along with most other major cities is restricted by a residence permit (*propiska*) system, designed to control inward migration and hence city size, in the face of their tendency to expand in response to industrial growth. (That such a conflict exists in a centrally planned society is explained by the fact that the ministries and their enterprises responsible for production may favour location in large

a. Greater Moscow

Ring road

0 km 10

Built-up area in 1917
Built-up since 1917 prox.)
Major industrial areas

Moskva R.

b. Urban infrastructure

High

Low

0 km 10

c. Urban character

High

Low

d. Residential character

High

Low

78

Fig. 5.3 Aspects of the spatial structure of Moscow. *Sources*: (b) Smith (1982a), Fig. 2, courtesy N.B. Barbash; (c) and (d) Barbash and Gutnov (1980), Figs. 4 and 5. Note that the shape of Moscow on Soviet maps is subject to some variation in scale and direction; those shown have followed the original sources.

cities on the grounds of economies of scale. Yet this places a further burden on what can be an already strained urban infrastructure which is the responsibility of the local city government or *soviet* to provide. One of the roles of the state and its Communist Party apparatus is to try to reconcile such problems.) To restrict the size of Moscow is a long-standing planning objective (see Hamilton, 1976; Hall, 1984, Chapter 5), but its continuing expansion is indicated not only by population growth of about 100,000 a year but also by steady extension of the built-up area. Most of the land within the ring road that defines the city limits is now built on or preserved as open space and there are a series of satellite towns beyond (Fig. 5.3a).

The approach to be adopted to the understanding of inequality in Moscow is different from that employed in the previous chapter. While aspects of areal differentiation and spatial organisation will be alluded to where relevant, we will proceed more directly than in the case of Atlanta to examine the interdependence of spatial form and social structure. The available data do not permit presentation of the kind of pattern of unequal living standards which figures on income (and other conditions) made possible in Atlanta. Instead, we will attempt to reveal the sources of inequality which arise from the process of socialist development sketched out in Fig. 5.1, so as to elaborate some of the structural contradictions of contemporary Soviet society outlined earlier in this chapter, though more thorough treatment will require recourse to specialised texts (e.g. French and Hamilton, 1979; Bater, 1980; Andrusz, 1984; Morton and Stuart, 1984; also Smith, 1979, Chapters 5 and 6).

There are a number of reasons to expect something approaching spatial equality of living standards in the Soviet city. As in the USA, inequality within the city can hardly be expected to arise from the uneven natural resource endowment which is responsible to some extent for variation in living standards at the regional scale under socialism as well as capitalism. And the market mechanisms which generate such an uneven distribution of income and so much that goes with it in the capitalist city are either eliminated or substantially under state control in the Soviet Union. Indeed, central appropriation of productive output, along with the planned provision of collective consumption in pursuit of equalitarian objectives, should in principal be a prescription for the abolition of inequality other than that permitted by private consumption from unequal personal incomes. The provision of collective consumption, including housing, is closely related to the physical structure and spatial organisation of Moscow; ever since 1917 urban planning has been a major instrument for the creation of a new society.

Most of Moscow is a product of the post-Revolutionary era (Fig. 5.3a), and even those quarters pre-dating 1917 are subject to partial reconstruction or renewal. The basic building block of the Soviet city is the *microraion* (micro-region or district). These are planned neighbourhoods for perhaps 5,000 to 15,000 people, comprising apartment blocks and day-to-day services in the form of restaurants, nurseries, kindergartens, club rooms, libraries and sports facilities, as well as education, health, retail and cultural services. The provision of collective consumption is usually on a per capita basis involving specific norms for the number of restaurant seats, square metres of shopping space and health service personnel, for example. If these norms are fulfilled, then everyone should have access to the same level of services within reasonable (generally walking) distance. Thus a wide range of human needs can be satisfied locally on an equal basis, subject only to trivial differences of physical access depending on where facilities are situated in relation to residence.

However, not all services can be close at hand for all people. Under the resource constraints which operate in even the most affluent society (which the USSR certainly is not), everyone cannot have a doctor, dentist, supermarket and cinema on the doorstep – far less a hospital with the full range of specialists, a department store or the Bolshoi Theatre. The *microraion* is in fact part of a nested hierarchy of service provision, involving successively larger clusters incorporating the level of retail, educational, medical, cultural and recreational facilities appropriate by the prevailing norms for successively larger groups of people. Thus the 'polyclinic' providing basic outpatient health care may serve three *microraion* populations of 20,000–50,000, with district hospitals catering for about 300,000 and major specialist hospitals in each of the eight zones into which the city is divided for health service planning. There will be shops providing for day-to-day food needs in every *microraion*, department stores stocking furniture and clothing further apart, and only a few highly specialised outlets for such items as scientific books and recorded music.

A carefully contrived spatial hierarchy after the fashion of Cristaller's central-place structure is the most effective means of optimising the access of a city's population to services, some of which are needed less frequently and can be provided less widely than others. But this is obviously not a prescription for perfect equality. And in so far as there may be a tendency to concentrate services in larger units on the grounds of efficiency (as appears to be the case in health care in Moscow), then there is an increasing conflict with the principle of equity manifest in equality of access, if only because it will take some people in some places longer to get to the more centralised specialist services than others elsewhere. The cost of public transport in Moscow is minimal (a few pence for a journey anywhere in the city), but the time, inconvenience and discomfort of a congested system exact a further price.

The hierarchical structure of service provision, along with a tendency for the larger, better and unique facilities (like the Bolshoi) to be in the city centre, means that in general the inner parts of Moscow are better provided for than the outer areas. This distinction is accentuated by the greater density of public transport routes in the inner city, which eases access to facilities elsewhere. There are also time lags in the construction of service facilities in the newer and outer residential areas, often years behind the completion of the housing blocks.

Some evidence as to the pattern of areal differentiation in service provision is provided in Fig. 5.3b. This shows the twenty-eight regions into which Moscow is divided for administrative purposes, shaded according to an index of urban infrastructure reflecting density of public transport lines and metro stations and of such facilities as laundries, shops, cafés, kindergartens, libraries and cinemas. The distinction between inner and outer regions is clear. A more detailed picture at a finer spatial scale (based on data for 423 tracts) is provided in Fig. 5.3c,

which shows an index of what the Soviet scholars responsible describe as 'urbanized character'. This combines information on 'the degree of physical development of the urban environment and the duration of its evolution'; tracts with high values are 'distinguished by the presence of theatres, a built-up area in keeping with Moscow's prominence as the nation's capital, a well-rounded urban environment and a high density of retail outlets selling manufactured goods' (Barbash and Gutnov, 1980, 567–8). In short, such tracts combine various desirable attributes of locality associated with the provision of means of collective consumption. They are concentrated in the central part of the city, with outliers in places where major transport nodes ensure good access from other parts of the metropolis.

The next step is to relate this pattern of service availability to residential space. Figure 5.3d is taken from the same study by Barbash and Gutnov and shows the extent of the residential character of Moscow by tracts by means of an index largely reflecting housing density. Those parts of the city which are most highly residential tend to be the extensive outer areas built since 1960, but they also include inner areas of pre-1917 or early post-Revolutionary construction. The inner residential areas clearly have advantages with respect to access to the service infrastructure of the city, but is this offset by poorer housing and associated features of the environment as it would be in a capitalist city?

The differentiation of housing quality is an intriguing feature of the Soviet city. To many visitors familiar with the diversity of urban landscape in Britain or the USA, and with the extent to which housing is a conspicuous indicator of the status of neighbourhoods and those who inhabit them, the impression of Moscow is one of uniformity to the point of monotony. And uniformity implies equality. In principle Soviet citizens are entitled to accommodation at a specific space norm per capita, for a rental payment originally fixed in 1928 and now less than 5 per cent of a family's income. In practice, however, inequality arises from qualitative differentiation of the housing stock, which is not reflected in cost or rent as it would be under market conditions, and which displays a geographical pattern different from that of the typical advanced capitalist city.

Housing tenure in the USSR divides roughly into three-quarters 'socialised' and one-quarter privately owner-occupied. Private housing is largely associated with the countryside and small towns, and tends to be of poor quality by conventional (state) standards, usually of a single-storey, timber construction often lacking some basic amenities. These physical defects, along with the association of private housing with individualistic values contrary to the official collectivist ideology, has led to the widespread clearance of this form of tenure in more recent years. In general, the larger the city the more private housing has been replaced by the landscape of the apartment block and *microraion*. Very little of this kind of housing survives in Moscow; it is mainly in small rural enclaves around the city fringe.

The socialised housing sector can be divided into three parts: local government, industrial and co-operative. About 60 per cent of housing in Moscow has been constructed and is owned by the city government, including most of that associated with *microraion* planning. About a quarter is owned by industrial and other ministries, their subordinate enterprises and other non-municipal authorities. While ministries and enterprises may have an incentive to provide good-quality housing (and often services such as health care at the place of work) so as to recruit and maintain an effective labour force, such conditions could be offset by high levels of pollution and other environmental disadvantages of housing often built in close proximity to factories. But period of construction seems more likely to be a source of differentiation in housing stock than the institution responsible for it. In general, newer housing will tend to be better, not only because of deterioration over time but also as a reflection of rising standards of space, fittings and finish. However, some early post-Revolutionary blocks were built to high standards and their inner-city location provides an especially attractive combination of attributes. Pre-Revolutionary (inner-city) housing, where it survives, can also be of high quality – or quite the reverse if subdivided and deteriorating in an old industrial area. Thus there is considerable scope for inequality in housing provision within the state sector.

The third element, co-operative housing, has a special significance, with respect to type of tenure as well as quality of accommodation. Co-operative housing is constructed on behalf of groups of individuals, usually based on the association of workplace (e.g. a particular enterprise or ministry), who thereby acquire collective ownership of their complex or block. Membership requires an initial monetary deposit, which can be considerable, and monthly payments about two-and-a-half times greater than the rent for the state apartment. Co-operative housing is concentrated in the largest cities of the Soviet Union with little in the rural area. It accounts for just over 8 per cent of all housing in Moscow, or a population of about 700,000. While it tends not to be conspicuously different from state housing in external appearances, co-operative housing is usually built to higher standards. Access to co-operative housing is a major source of inequality in the

Soviet city, the more so in Moscow where its development has been greatest. Its significance is summarised as follows by Andrusz (1984, 94):

> . . . the co-operative member will first of all consider himself to be lucky in having been accepted into a co-operative since more people want to join than there are places available. Secondly, he will regard being a member as a privilege in the sense that he is a member of a minority tenure group and thereby distinguished from people living in other housing tenures. (Membership of a house-building co-operative might have the same social significance as living on a particular private housing estate or in a postal district in Britain.) Thirdly, his privileged status will be regarded as such by a large number of non-residents.

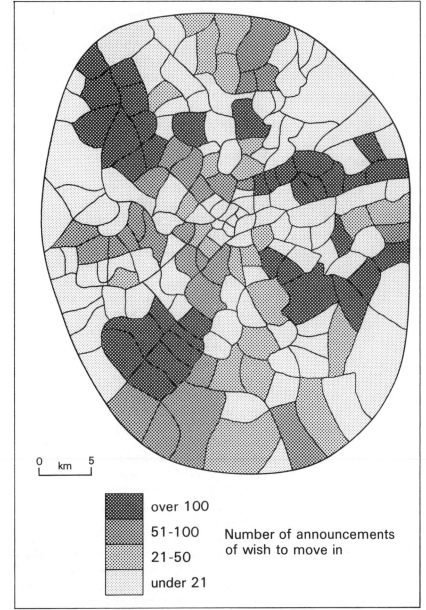

Fig. 5.4 Relative residential attraction of different parts of Moscow, as indicated by number of people announcing a wish to move in by exchanging their present apartment for one of the same size. *Source*: Barbash (1984), Fig. 1.

0 km 5

over 100

51-100   Number of announcements
21-50   of wish to move in
under 21

In short, being in a house-building co-operative is a symbol of status, connected largely with occupation and income, and having an association with place.

These observations lead to the broader question of the relationship between local environmental quality, housing tenure, social groups and geographical location. Within the capitalist city an essential ingredient in the formation of patterns of association among these conditions is the exercise of residential choice, within the constraints of the housing market. There is some freedom of choice in Moscow, even in the state (socialised) sector, through the exchange of apartments facilitated by advertisements in a newspaper published for this purpose. Figure 5.4 shows the pattern revealed by a recent analysis of announcement of wishes to move into different parts of the city, involving only apartments of the size currently occupied so as to isolate the element of locational choice. While it must be recognised that some of the fringe comprises open space and would not therefore attract potential residents, there is nevertheless a suggestion of distinct wedges of preferred space, notably in the south west and north west. Some inner areas also seem attractive to Muscovites seeking a change of residence.

Evidence concerning the congregation of social groups within particular parts of Moscow is hard to find. However, some indication of differences in local occupational structure is provided by Fig. 5.5. This is part of a study by Barbash (1983a), in which twenty-four areas in Moscow with contrasting environments were selected for an analysis of child health. Data were acquired from the polyclinics serving these areas, for more than 5,000 babies born in 1978, and the map shows the occupational status of the mothers. The differences in local occupational structure are highlighted by the varying proportions of material production (i.e. factory) workers, compared with specialists and students. Most notable is the contrast between the two south-eastern areas in the heavily industrial district beside the river and the area in the south-western wedge with a much smaller proportion of workers in material production and more specialists and students. This south-western segment of the city, along Leninsky Prospekt and out to the city fringe, is clearly one of relatively high socio-economic status, with a concentration of co-operative apartments, and is sharply differentiated in environmental quality from the sector to the east with its evidently industrial landscape and high levels of pollution. That both social structure and local environmental quality may be reflected in other aspects of living standards is suggested by the finding of Barbash (1983b) that illness among young children is highest in those districts where the proportion of women who are workers (as opposed to specialists) or housewives (single-income families) is highest.

The most extreme manifestation of inequality in Moscow is provided by the privileges accorded to those who hold the highest positions of power and influence. This elite comprises the upper levels in political, military, academic and artistic life. In addition to high incomes, individuals (and their families) occupying these key roles receive more subtle and often non-material benefits including access to goods (e.g. from the West) not usually available to ordinary citizens and special services such as the so-called Kremlin Clinic for senior political figures and a hospital set aside for members of the Soviet Academy of Sciences.

Fig. 5.5 Socio-economic structure of selected parts of Moscow, as indicated by occupation of mothers of babies recorded at local polyclinics. *Source*: Barbash (1983a)75.

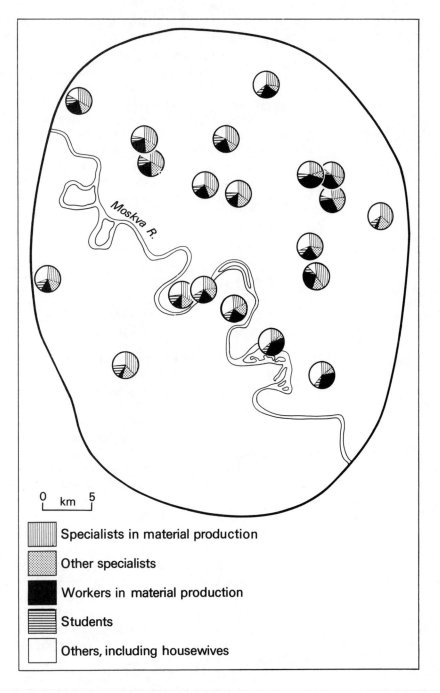

0 km 5

	Specialists in material production
	Other specialists
	Workers in material production
	Students
	Others, including housewives

Elite status can also influence access to education, such as a place for one's child in Moscow State University or some such prestigious institution, which in its turn can lead to a high-status occupation and perhaps incorporation into the next generation of the elite.

One of the most important privileges of the elite is access to superior housing. There are blocks of apartments in Moscow which serve this purpose. They are usually in a fairly central location and include modern buildings and some older ones built for the pre-Revolutionary bourgeoisie and renovated to a high standard, as well as the 'wedding cake' towers of the Stalin era which are conspicuous features of the inner-city skyline. Housing for the elite also includes what can be substantial country houses or *dachas* outside the city.

Elite privilege is part of the incentive system that seeks to ensure the reproduction of Soviet society through recruitment of suitable individuals into key roles. Such roles themselves arise from the necessity for central control of economic and cultural life. But herein lies an important contradiction: because privilege conflicts with the state ideology of egalitarianism it must be inconspicuous, yet well enough known to serve the purpose of inducements. Luxury consumption and extravagant life styles can be confined largely to the privacy of the home, the internal splendours of which may be disguised by a bland exterior or a location deep in the woodlands beyond the city limits. Within the city, individual buildings may stand out, though localised concentrations of the elite as opposed to the relatively well-to-do co-operative dwellers are hard to identify. Nevertheless, few Muscovites can be unaware of what one informant describes as 'special places for special people'.

Spatial form and social process

The main points of this account of the spatial expression of inequality in Moscow may now be related, briefly, to some elements of social structure identified earlier in this chapter, and hence to the central theme of the mutual interdependence of space of society. The form of socio-economic differentiation (inequality) in the city may be summarised as follows. The inner areas present a variety of environmental and social groups, with some good housing which combines with access to cultural facilities to generate what may to most people be the best of all worlds in Moscow, other than that of the discrete enclaves of the elite (including the Soviet version of 'gentrification' of deteriorated older property originally built to superior standards). In contrast, there are the remains of the poor inner-city housing areas, less substantial than in other Soviet cities and occupied by people of markedly lower status than the intelligentsia and 'professional' groups that tend to predominate in the inner city. The outer areas are differentiated by wedges of varying environmental quality and socio-economic status of the population, with the better sectors having relatively high proportions of co-operative housing and the occupations that tend to go with it, the inhabitants trading off the higher levels of access to cultural facilities, shopping and other services in the city centre for new housing of good quality and proximity to open space on the edge of the city. In the sectors where state housing predominates, environmental quality will be better than in those older, inner areas occupied by people of lower occupational status, except for access to services, but there may be high crime and other social pathologies associated with lack of a sense of community and, for recent migrants, difficulty adjusting to city life (Morton and Stuart, 1984, 122–3). Beyond the city limits are the *dachas,* satellite towns and areas of private housing sending perhaps 500,000 commuters into Moscow daily.

These indications of spatial social stratification clearly conflict with the ideal of a socialist city planned to foster equalitarianism. There are forces at work generating a spatial form which may frustrate the purpose expressed in the largely self-contained *microraion* as a drawing-board and concrete expression of the capacity of urban design to mould human conduct. Andrusz (1984, 5) makes the point:

> High rise, high density, publicly (or co-operatively) owned housing may be a requisite for the pursuit of some sort of 'collectivist ideal' – an ideal that permeates Soviet Marxism. Yet such an ideal conflicts with a dominant trend in Soviet social life – towards a more privatised way of life arising from increased personal mobility, rising car ownership, a falling birth rate and nuclearisation of the family.

Personal mobility is especially important in a city the size of Moscow. At the end of the 1960s there were only 100,000 cars in Moscow; now there are over a million. All this extends people's social networks beyond the immediate residential locality or workplace, while the growing privatisation of consumption associated with increasing prosperity and the inclination to ape capitalist materialism encourages a consolidation of home and family as the primary unit of association and socialisation. What is lost is the collectivism, supposedly fostered by the communal life of the apartment block or *microraion*.

Social-spatial stratification thus reflects individual behaviour as people seek personal advantage within the structure and spatial form of Soviet society. Freedom to choose is related to an incentive system based on the division of labour: those who are better paid and better educated arrange their lives to what they see as their best advantage. And there may be further important changes to come, with Gorbachov's 'reforms', including differential rentals in the state housing sector encouraging further spatial sorting and even migration of skilled workers and those in high-status or elite occupations to permanent residence beyond the city limits and suburban car commuting as in the West (Andrusz, 1984, 269, 278).

Conclusion

The crucial significance of this case study is that a spatial form of inequality is emerging from the structural features of a supposedly equalitarian society, a form which itself feeds back into social process (in the manner suggested in Fig. 5.1). The outcome may be further social/spatial differentiation, as (privileged) group identity is reinforced by geographical propinquity and separation from other sections of the population. This group advantage may be reproduced and perpetuated, just as Smith (1986) suggests that the 'urban specialist class' and others have a vested interest in maintaining the privilege of place associated with restricted access to cities in general. Consolidation of such patterns of differentiation, albeit subject to changing forms over time, seems certain further to frustrate whatever residual tendencies there may be in Soviet socialism to complete its already lengthy transition to full communism. But it is just as certain that the spatial expression of inequality, like the structure of Soviet society, will remain significantly different from that of capitalism. The existing built environment and the patterns of life developed within it will ensure that Atlanta and Moscow continue to be conspicuously different cities.

6 Inequality under apartheid: the case of South Africa

No country in the world evokes inequality quite like South Africa. Furthermore, the racial inequality associated with apartheid is widely regarded as unjust. The theme of social justice has not been touched on since its introduction in the first chapter of this book: understanding inequality has been task enough, without attempting to tackle equity. Indeed, it has been strongly implied if not stated directly that some form of inequality is a necessary accompaniment of particular kinds of society, whether between the rich and poor under capitalism or the elite and the mass of the people under socialism. While the degree of inequality in any society may be capable of some reduction by government action, to say that the basic form of inequality observable in the USA or USSR, for example, is unjust is to judge the system generating it. It is far from self-evident that inequality expressed racially, as under apartheid, is more of a moral problem than inequality by class or occupation group. Racial inequality may appear more arbitrary – less clearly related to reward for services rendered than inequality arising from role in the economy, society or polity – and thus more easily condemned. But it may nevertheless be integral to the structure of a society and instrumental in its ongoing reproduction, hence explicable if not justifiable in these terms.

The intention here is not to make a moral judgement on apartheid, but to assist the understanding required, among other things, to sustain such judgement on the part of those who may wish to do so. It will be shown in this chapter that South African society is more complicated than is often supposed: that although apartheid is synonymous with racial inequality it is not simply a case of political domination and repression based on white antipathy towards blacks. There is an important economic dimension to apartheid, related to the fact that South Africa's predominant mode of production is capitalist and that this thrives on cheap labour. Above all, it will be stressed that geographical space is intrinsic to apartheid: the word itself means 'separation' in the language of Afrikaans. Indeed apartheid could be described as the most ambitious exercise in applied geography in the contemporary world. The approach will be consistent with that adopted in the other case studies, revealing the mutual interdependence of social structure and spatial form. The distinctive circumstances of South Africa will in fact help to highlight certain features of this relationship. The primary expression of inequality in South Africa is so evidently racial that its geographical pattern is of no special interest. But spatial organisation is crucial to the maintenance of black subordination, in both the political and economic sphere. This may then feed back into social process, constraining change in some ways and encouraging it in others. Pressure points are arising in particular places, associated with some of the contradictions inherent in the social and spatial structure of apartheid, and their violent eruption is part of the process whereby a new kind of society may eventually be formed.

To fill out the main points of this argument requires the full attention of this chapter. Further background to apartheid and its geographical basis in South Africa can be found elsewhere (Omond, 1986; Smith, 1982b, 1987), and in a text which sets the country in the broader framework of development studies (Fair, 1982).

Racial inequality

South Africa has a total population (1984) of over 32.6 million. The people are officially classified into four primary race groups: the Blacks, i.e. negroes, comprising 24.1 million or 73.8 per cent of the total; the Whites, of European descent, 4.8 million (14.8 per cent); the Coloureds, of 'mixed' blood, 2.8 million (8.7 per cent); and the Asians, mostly of Indian descent, 0.9 million (2.7 per cent).

The Blacks are subdivided into ten major tribal groups. The most numerous are the Zulu with about 5.5 million at the 1980 census, or more than the entire White population, and the Xhosa (4.2 million), followed by the North Sotho, the Tswana and the South Sotho, each with around 2 million. The Whites divide roughly into 60 per cent Afrikaners (mainly of Dutch and German origin) by the criterion of Afrikaans being their first language, and 40 per cent of English background. Unlike the 'expatriate' Whites usually associated with colonialism, the Afrikaners have become separated from their European origin linguistically and in some cultural respects, and regard South Africa as their permanent home occupied virtually by divine right.

Racial nomenclature is complicated in South Africa by some subtlety of usage. The Blacks, formerly known officially as the Bantu, are often referred to as Africans in recognition of the fact that they alone are indigenous to the continent of Africa. The Blacks/Africans, Coloureds and Asians are increasingly identified collectively as 'blacks', to evoke a trans-racial solidarity and to avoid the negative connotations of 'non-white' (the capital letter B is adopted in what follows to distinguish Blacks in the narrower official sense from the wider term). But whatever the labels placed on groups of people according to skin pigmentation, the Whites are in quite a small minority when compared with the numerically dominant Blacks, the more so when the Coloureds and Asians are included.

The Whites nevertheless appropriate most of the wealth in South Africa. The highly unequal distribution of income compared with population was illustrated in the first chapter (Fig. 1.2). Table 6.1 shows up-to-date figures on some other economic and social indicators by race, with the ratio of advantage of Whites compared with Blacks as a measure of degree of inequality. Average annual earnings in occupations other than agriculture and domestic service show the Whites almost four times better off than the Blacks, with the Coloureds between the Blacks and Asians. Average household income reveals a greater gap between Blacks and Whites, explained by the proportion of Blacks in poorly paid agricultural and domestic jobs; the fact that Black household income is less than average earnings also reflects the number of Blacks unemployed or in the traditional largely subsistence sector of the economy. Per capita expenditure on pensions (for which many Blacks do not qualify) and for education show some difference in degree of inequality and relativities among the race groups. The infant mortality figures are probably a substantial underestimate for Blacks; they underline the low living standard of the Coloureds with a figure similar to that of Mexico and the Philippines. Finally, a Black or Coloured was six times more likely to be shot by the police in 1984 than a White or a member of the Asian group, which has not thus far revealed much inclination for violent confrontation with the forces of the state.

Table 6.1 Selected economic and social indicators by race group in South Africa.

Indicator	Blacks (B)	Whites (W)	Coloureds	Asians	W:B
Average annual earnings (R) 1983	3,720	14,520	5,004	7,008	3.90
Average household income (R) 1984	3,276	22,008	7,488	12,864	6.72
Annual expenditure on old-age pensions/ capita (R) 1982–3	569	1,664	960	985	2.92
Educational expenditure/ capita (R) 1983–4	234	1,654	569	1,088	7.01
Infant deaths/1,000 live births 1982	80.0	13.4	59.2	20.7	5.97
Persons shot by police/ million population	43.3	7.3	49.1	9.0	5.93

Note: R = Rand; 3.1R = £1 sterling in 1986.
Source: *Survey of Race Relations 1984*, South African Institute of Race Relations, Johannesburg, 1985.

However high the degree of racial inequality in South Africa may be, there have been reductions in recent years. Table 6.2 shows the distribution of income at various dates since 1936 along with the coefficient of concentration as a measure of degree of inequality (explained in Chapter 1). There was not much change until the early 1970s, when labour unrest prompted considerable increases in Black wages. The 1977 figures compared with the earlier ones show that all the other groups have improved their position relative to that of the Whites, and later figures for earnings confirm a continuation of the same trend. Another significant feature of these figures is the decreasing

Table 6.2 Percentage distribution of population (P) and income (I) by race group in South Africa 1936–77.

	Blacks		Whites		Coloureds		Asians		Coefficient of concentration
	P	I	P	I	P	I	P	I	
1936	68.8	19.7	20.9	74.5	8.0	4.1	2.3	1.7	53.6
1946/7	68.5	20.1	20.7	73.8	8.2	4.2	2.3	1.9	53.1
1956/7	68.0	20.6	19.9	72.5	9.1	4.8	2.9	2.0	52.6
1967	69.4	18.8	18.2	73.4	9.5	5.4	2.9	2.4	55.2
1970/1	70.0	19.1	17.7	73.6	9.4	5.2	2.9	2.1	55.9
1977	71.9	25.5	16.2	64.0	9.1	7.3	2.8	3.2	48.2

Source: Smith (1977) Table 9.4, except 1977 from *Survey of Race Relations 1978*, South African Institute of Race Relations, Johannesburg, 1979.

proportion of the total population accounted for by Whites.

All inequality is not capable of identification in numerical terms. An important aspect of apartheid is the unequal treatment of different race groups with respect to access to 'public' services and facilities and to participation in social, cultural and sporting life. This form of discrimination is referred to as 'petty' apartheid, to distinguish it from (grand) apartheid expressed in the planned subdivision of national and urban space on racial grounds, to be explained below. The indignity of being treated in a different and usually inferior manner if of dark skin is an important and continuing feature of inequality under apartheid.

Spatial and structural relations

Apartheid and the inequalities that it sustains is not arbitrary racial discrimination but the result of deliberate state policy. The dual imperatives of the South African government are the preservation of White rule and the privilege that goes with it, and the perpetuation of a profitable capitalist economy. In so far as White power is perceived as a matter of survival, physical and cultural, it has a priority claim on resources which may conflict with expanded reproduction in the form of economic growth. Apartheid is expensive to maintain, and constrains economic development not only because upholding it diverts part of the surplus from investment but also through the rigid control of Blacks which may frustrate the more efficient use of their labour. Despite these contradictions, the state's political and economic objectives largely reinforce one another, with the White government dedicated to capitalism and capitalist business at home and overseas tending to be supportive of White rule if not always enthusiastic about the way apartheid operates. The most important structural feature connecting the political and economic spheres in South Africa is the status of Blacks as predominantly cheap and disenfranchised labour. And a crucial instrument for maintaining this is spatial organisation.

Understanding the background to 'grand' apartheid requires a brief historical excursion. The first Dutch settlement at Cape Town began in 1652, but it was British occupation of the Cape at the beginning of the eighteenth century and their immigration to Natal which really consolidated White control of South Africa. Disenchantment with British rule led to the Great Trek which took the Boer descendants of the Dutch settlers into the interior. Their encounters with the indigenous African population led to violent struggles which have left a deep impression on Afrikaner culture and politics, including an insistence on the right continually to occupy and rule the southern tip of this continent in the face of all opposition. The Africans were defeated, and firmly contained within tribal reserves. The discovery of gold on the Witwatersrand in the 1880s soon shifted the economic centre of gravity from the coast (especially Cape Town and Durban) to the emerging city of Johannesburg, to which Africans were steadily drawn as migrant labour; they eventually became permanent residents of 'townships' built for this purpose. The Coloured population found largely in the western Cape Province, and the immigration of Indians mostly to work in the Natal sugar fields from the late nineteenth century onwards, completed the primary race groups.

Since the conflict of the Boer War between the descendants of the Dutch and English settlers, the identity of these two sections of the White population has tended to become blurred. The election of the predominantly Afrikaner National Party to power in 1948 nevertheless represented an important political change. The Nationalists soon set about replacing the pragmatic racial domination and informal segregation of the past by the more clearly articulated and rigid policy of apartheid. Originally described as 'separate development', the policy involved the allocation, to each of the main African tribal groups, of a 'homeland' corresponding roughly with the original reserves, as well as the implementation of strict residential segregation in towns and cities through the designation of racially exclusive 'group areas'. The policy is now referred to by the South African government as 'multinationalism', with the homelands eventually becoming self-governing independent states for their respective tribal nationalities. The Coloureds and Asians were assigned neither votes nor homelands, though were given a form of parliamentary representation under constitutional 'reforms' in 1984.

Figure 6.1 shows the homelands, or Bantustans as they are sometimes called. Together they account for a little more than 13 per cent of the land area of South Africa, and for almost three-quarters of the total population. Four are now 'independent republics' in government parlance, though they are not recognised as such by the outside world. The others remain Black 'national states' within the Republic of South Africa. The planned independence of all ten would leave a residual White republic. The official rationale for this policy is that spatial separation is the best way to avoid conflict and to protect the aspirations of all groups in multiracial society. Within their own national territory the Blacks will have the same rights as the Whites in their nation; to quote former Prime Minister B.J. Vorster, 'If I were to wake up one morning and find myself a Black man, the only major difference would be geographical' (*Johannesburg Star*, 3 April 1973).

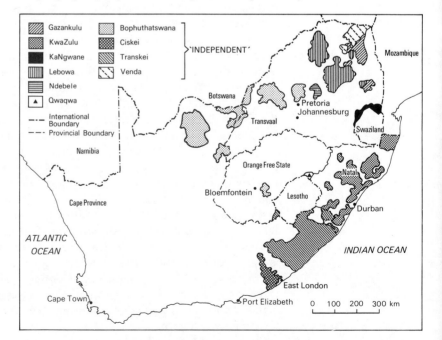

Fig. 6.1 South Africa's Black homelands, distinguishing between the 'independent republics' and 'national states'. *Source*: Smith (1987), Fig. 1.1.

However, the actual geographical disposition of the homelands suggests a different purpose. Not only do they divide the Blacks as a group into ten nations, but most of these are themselves fragmented geographically. Together with the absence of major towns and natural resources other than people and land, both usually poor, this means that the basis for viable nation states does not exist. A more plausible interpretation is that they serve the purpose of divide and rule, in a spatial reorganisation of South Africa planned for the preservation of White rule, under a capitalist mode of production, via the maintenance of the Black population as disenfranchised and cheap labour.

How the political objective is achieved is quite straightforward. About half the Black population (over 10 million) actually live in 'white' South Africa outside the homelands, but if they are deemed to be citizens of a homeland this transfers their political rights to places where they pose no real threat to White power where it matters. The loss of some territory from the original Republic is of little consequence: the economic heartland centred on the Witwatersrand, along with all other major towns and cities, remains 'white'.

The economics of apartheid is rather more complicated. The maintenance of White rule, facilitated by the homeland policy, contributes to the perpetuation of cheap (Black) labour in some indirect ways. For example, Black trade unions can be restricted, and activists pressing for better wages and living conditions for Blacks can be banished to their supposed national territory. But market forces play their part, for there is an abundance of Black labour in the rapidly increasing population to keep the price down. In the normal circumstances of a competitive capitalist economy with free mobility of labour, Blacks would leave the peripheral areas in large numbers and flood the cities seeking work, thus threatening social stability. However, the South African government has sought to impose order on both the labour market and the process of urbanisation, using a system of influx control to limit Black access to the cities to those for whom employment is available. The spatial organisation of apartheid is crucial to this strategy.

Black labour enters the 'white' economy in three distinct geographical forms (Table 6.3). The first and most numerous is the permanent resident workforce, living in townships such as Soweto on the edge of Johannesburg. This form has the advantage of being close at hand in relation to places of work, as would be expected in a

Table 6.3   Spatial forms of Black African labour in 'white' South Africa, 1982–3.

Spatial form	Numbers (million) (approx.)
Permanent residents	3.50
Migrants: from homelands	1.40
from foreign countries	0.36
Frontier commuters	0.77
Total	6.00

Source: based on figures in *Race Relations Survey 1984*, South African Institute of Race Relations, Johannesburg, 1985, and *South Africa 1985*, Official Yearbook of the Republic of South Africa, Department of Foreign Affairs, Pretoria.

conventional industrial city, although in South Africa it is in a peripheral rather than a central location. However, permanent Black residence is a conspicuous contradiction to the homeland policy – a constant reminder that millions of Blacks are disenfranchised where they actually live and work – and a potential and at times real threat to social control. It is therefore state policy to restrict permanent Black residences in 'white' South Africa as far as possible.

The second form of Black labour is migrant labour, originally fostered by the mining industry, with workers coming on usually a year's contract from their homeland or a country beyond South Africa's borders. Such labour is cheap because wages do not have to cover the cost of supporting the family left behind, or indeed the worker him- or herself when between contracts, unemployed or retired, for the area of origin is expected to perform this function. The homelands or tribal reserves in South Africa thus relieve the 'white' capitalist economy of a substantial part of the cost of production and ongoing reproduction of its migrant labour force. However, this role is increasingly threatened by the breakdown of the traditional pre-capitalist mode of production in the homeland, which sustains the migrant labour system by supporting workers when at home and their families much of the time. Furthermore, separating workers from their families is increasingly criticised on humanitarian grounds, and migrants are in any event inconvenient as a basis for a sophisticated economy dependent on a reliable supply of increasingly skilled labour.

The third geographical form of labour is the frontier commuter. This is a distinctive creation of apartheid, which involves the daily movement of workers from townships in the homelands to nearby adjoining 'white' cities. This combines the most advantageous features of the two other labour forces, in so far as capital is concerned. The labour is conveniently close, like the permanent residents, yet beyond what is or should eventually become an international boundary. Political aspirations are expected to be satisfied in the homeland nation state or independent republic, which also relieves the 'white' Republic of direct responsibility for the social services, urban infrastructure and other costs associated with the production and reproduction of labour. The growing importance of frontier commuters is indicated by an increase from 290,000 in 1970 to 773,000 in 1982, compared with 1,460,000 to 1,753,000 in the number of migrant workers.

Figure 6.2 illustrates something of the spatial form of the city most closely associated with frontier commuting. Durban has a population of 960,000 (1980 census), including 320,000 Whites, 468,000 Asians or Indians, 56,000 Coloureds and 116,000 Blacks/Africans. The map shows the main group areas for Whites and Indians within the city and the small Black townships. Beyond the city limits, the homeland of KwaZulu, are two much larger townships of Umlazi and Kwa Mashu, responsible for the vast majority of the 400,000 or so commuters from KwaZulu into 'white' South Africa. Physically and economically, these two townships are an integral part of the Durban metropolis, but defined politically as part of a Black nation state. The other major venue for frontier commuters is Pretoria, which receives most of the almost 200,000 leaving 'independent' Bophuthatswana, the border of which is only about ten miles from the city. The Witwatersrand and

Fig. 6.2 The Durban metropolitan area, showing race group areas and Black townships within the homeland of KwaZulu. *Source*: based on Smith (1987), Fig. 1.3.

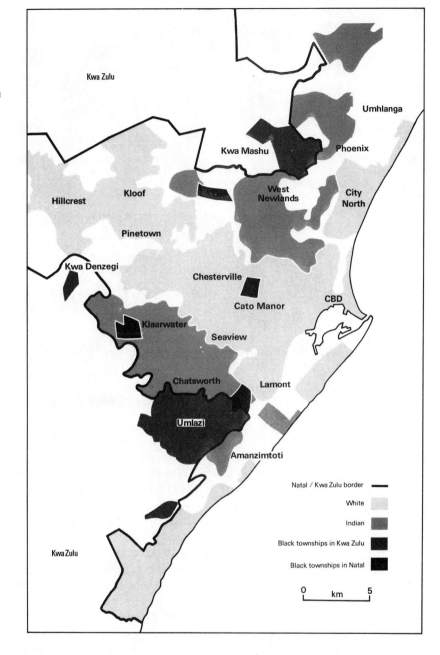

Cape Town are too far from homelands for frontier commuting and have to rely on permanent township residents or migrants for their Black labour; it is in these two areas that the geographical inconsistency of apartheid at the national scale is most clearly exposed.

This complex spatial organisation of Black labour supply arises from different attempts to resolve the basic contradiction of the South African political economy: the need for Black labour without conceding the vote and other commonly accepted rights that go with citizenship. The ideology of racism allows Blacks to be seen as different from and inferior to others, in some respects as less than fully human, and this is held to justify different and unequal treatment. Spatial organisation is

Housing contrasts in Cape Town: home of well-to-do Whites near Table Mountain, well protected from the less well-off (top); Crossroads, the large spontaneous settlement where Blacks defied the White authorities for years – and where open warfare between conservatives and radicals broke out in 1986 (bottom).

as close as it is possible to get to the separation of the physical capacity to labour from its human embodiment. This distinction was vividly expressed by a Nationalist member of parliament who said of the Blacks some years ago: 'They are only supplying a commodity, the commodity of labour . . . it is labour we are importing and not labourers as individuals'.

A particular spatial form of political jurisdiction, labour supply and urbanisation has thus been created by the state, in an attempt to ensure the reproduction of a structure of society characterised by minority White control and a capitalist economy thriving on cheap Black labour. Thus far the strategy has been largely successful, in its own terms. However, spatial form feeds back into social process with sometimes unintended and perhaps unwelcome consequences, as the South African government is discovering. And despite the strength of state control, the Blacks (and Coloureds and Asians) are not passively accepting the role and place assigned to them in the structure of apartheid society; they are becoming active agents in both social and spatial change. The most obvious physical expression of these tendencies is the growth of spontaneous or 'squatter' settlements around many South African cities, exemplified by Crossroads on the edge of Cape Town. There are probably more than 3 million blacks, mainly Africans, living in spontaneous settlements in South Africa today, despite rigid influx controls which make most of them illegal. Spontaneous settlements reflect not only a shortage of housing for blacks but also a mismatch between the availability of urban space and demand for it on the part of those Blacks/Africans who wish to seek work away from the desperate poverty of the homelands. These settlements are not on the scale found in some other African countries or in parts of Latin America and South East Asia, but they do reveal limitations of capacity of the state to mould urbanisation to its own purpose, and demonstrate the power of the Black people themselves to play a more positive part in the creation of their own environments. And from this comes a growing confidence to engage even more actively in the creation of a new society.

Place, conflict and change

In the first chapter of this book some reference was made to the role of violence in social change. Such conduct conventionally elicits disapproval, not only on the part of those whose security is thereby threatened but also because violence is discordant with the liberal Christian tradition which places faith in peaceful change. However, those who are terrorists to some are freedom fighters to others and to fight for freedom is often applauded. The history of human society is one in which violent conflict has frequently been required both to promote and to resist change. This is not to condone violence, but to recognise reality. And as we showed in Chapter 1, violence tends not to be random and irrational but an outcome of the material conditions which people experience in specific places – whether in Watts, Brixton or Soweto.

The violence occurring day by day in South Africa in recent years has to be understood in this light, as an outcome of structural tensions which break out in particular kinds of places to effect subsequent change. It must also be seen as purposeful, not necessarily in the sense that those involved fully comprehend their own motivation and work consistently to obtain carefully contrived goals, but because it is clearly selective. The targets chosen and the local circumstances of violent conflict crystallise contradictions within the socio-spatial structure which individuals through their action seek to resolve.

Violent unrest usually takes the form of a group of Blacks or, less frequently, Coloureds, throwing stones at vehicles or attacking buildings with petrol bombs. The targets are usually associated with the forces of the state in the form of the South African police or defence force, or with institutions and individuals viewed as agents of repression. Schools are frequently attacked, sometimes by their own increasingly politicised students, as are the homes and vehicles of Black policemen and local councillors, and Coloured members of the new parliament have been similarly targeted. The police response is usually to move in with a demonstration of force, thus provoking further violent reaction, and to use shotguns resulting in injuries or death to demonstrators. Arrests are made, sometimes in large numbers.

The types of locations involved show that the pressure points are predominantly the Black townships in 'white' South Africa. These are the places of the permanent yet voteless residents, on whom capital depends so greatly for the relatively stable element of its labour, and White households for their domestic servants. They are places with long rows of small, overcrowded houses, unkempt and poorly lighted streets,

One day's 'unrest' in South Africa, as recorded in police reports reproduced in the *Cape Times*, 16 January 1986.

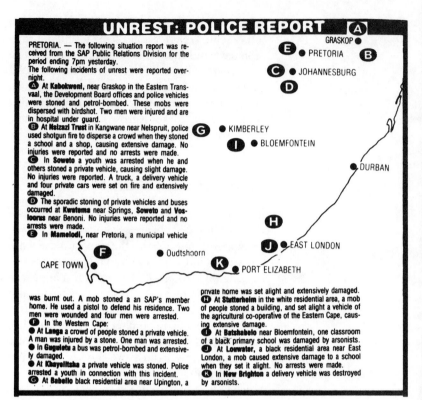

UNREST: POLICE REPORT

PRETORIA. — The following situation report was received from the SAP Public Relations Division for the period ending 7pm yesterday.
The following incidents of unrest were reported overnight.

Ⓐ At **Kabokweni**, near Graskop in the Eastern Transvaal, the Development Board offices and police vehicles were stoned and petrol-bombed. These mobs were dispersed with birdshot. Two men were injured and are in hospital under guard.

Ⓑ At **Natzazl Trust** in Kangwane near Nelspruit, police used shotgun fire to disperse a crowd when they stoned a school and a shop, causing extensive damage. No injuries were reported and no arrests were made.

Ⓒ In **Soweto** a youth was arrested when he and others stoned a private vehicle, causing slight damage. No injuries were reported. A truck, a delivery vehicle and four private cars were set on fire and extensively damaged.

Ⓓ The sporadic stoning of private vehicles and buses occurred at **Kwatema** near Springs, **Soweto** and **Vosloorus** near Benoni. No injuries were reported and no arrests were made.

Ⓔ In **Mamelodi**, near Pretoria, a municipal vehicle

GRASKOP ●
Ⓔ ● PRETORIA Ⓑ
Ⓒ ● JOHANNESBURG
Ⓓ

Ⓖ ● KIMBERLEY
Ⓘ ● BLOEMFONTEIN
● DURBAN
Ⓗ
Ⓙ ● EAST LONDON
Ⓕ ● Oudtshoorn
CAPE TOWN ● Ⓚ ● PORT ELIZABETH

was burnt out. A mob stoned a an SAP's member home. He used a pistol to defend his residence. Two men were wounded and four men were arrested.

Ⓕ In the Western Cape:
● At **Langa** a crowd of people stoned a private vehicle. A man was injured by a stone. One man was arrested.
● In **Guguletu** a bus was petrol-bombed and extensively damaged.
● At **Khayelitsha** a private vehicle was stoned. Police arrested a youth in connection with this incident.
Ⓖ At **Babello** black residential area near Upington, a

private home was set alight and extensively damaged.
Ⓗ At **Stutterheim** in the white residential area, a mob of people stoned a building, and set alight a vehicle of the agricultural co-operative of the Eastern Cape, causing extensive damage.
Ⓘ At **Batshabelo** near Bloemfontein, one classroom of a black primary school was damaged by arsonists.
Ⓙ At **Louwater**, a black residential area near East London, a mob caused extensive damage to a school when they set it alight. No arrests were made.
Ⓚ In **New Brighton** a delivery vehicle was destroyed by arsonists.

'shebeen' yards where drinking an illicit brew provides temporary escape from arduous labour and long journeys to work, and with the constant risk of robbery, rape and murder. These are the places where the major disturbances have taken place historically, from Sharpeville in 1960 to Soweto in 1976 and subsequently. The worst environments in a physical sense, in the spontaneous settlements, generated few incidents: here people are creating their own communities in a physical and social sense, with this and the constant threat of eviction and search for work exercising its own form of social control. However, Crossroads was overtaken by violence in 1986, as the more stable and conservative residents came into conflict with political radicals. Violence often finds its most brutal expression in mine compounds, among men living in dormitories away from their family but not integrated into urban life and with sufficient tribal loyalty for frustration to find expression in vicious faction fights. The Coloured areas in the Cape erupt periodically, with violence characteristic of that reported almost daily in the Black townships. The White places and people experience very little of the violence, and the Indians who are the best off in aggregate of the black groups even less.

But violence is not the only strategy of Black opposition. There have been successful boycotts of White business, strikes and other workplace resistance, and a growing political cohesion centred on the re-emergence of the African National Congress. The political target is not simply racism and White rule, but is increasingly incorporating the economic system and its often multinational corporation which are seen as profiting from racial oppression with little more than lip service to Black advancement unless prompted by commercial self-interest. Some commentators see 'a marked shift amongst black opinion – notably among students and in the trade union movement – in favour of an explicitly anti-capitalist position', with a socialist economic system seen as a better option (Bundy, 1986, 11).

This leads to the final reminder that South Africa is as it is not simply because of racism, from which it follows that the country's problems would not all be solved with the end of discrimination, or indeed the dismantling of apartheid. While racial antagonism and the ideology of White supremacy has roots deep in the historical and cultural experience of South Africa, as it has in the American South, it takes particular economic arrangements to generate inequality arising largely from access to resources. It is the social relations of capitalism allied to White power which keep Blacks along with most Coloureds and Asians in a state of poverty and subordination. In fact, race alone no longer defines economic status exclusively in South Africa, if it ever did in a land of tribal chiefs and Indian traders. There is a small property-owning bourgeoisie within the Coloured and Asian groups, to some extent deliberately fostered by the government as likely to be supportive of the status quo in the face of such alternatives as a 'radical' Black government. The Blacks are certainly not united in opposition to White rule, with the Asians in particular having the lesson of Amin's Uganda as a reminder of what Black African rule could mean. Some of the homelands provide even closer evidence that repressive and conservative government is not a sole prerogative of Whites. While it is fanciful at this stage to see a trans-racial working-class alliance confronting capital in some revolutionary scenario, the nature of South African society is being increasingly revealed as one of cleavage based on class as well as race. And this has a bearing on the process of change.

Conclusion

To speculate about South Africa's future is tempting but hazardous, the more so in a period of volatility. Our analysis should have helped to reveal some of the spatial and structural features of apartheid generating forces for change, but the likely trajectory is far from clear. It cannot be read from existing structures, even if they were perfectly understood, for it depends also on external events in global power politics. The only certainty is that the White government will not voluntarily dismantle apartheid, in the foreseeable future and probably not ever, for too much depends on it. Responsibility for future events rests crucially on individual South Africans, living out their lives as best they can within the prevailing structure and spatial organisation of society, assisting its reproduction by implicit compliance or driven by desperation and perhaps a vision of something better to demonstrate that even the most oppressed people are in some respects, in certain times and places, capable of taking charge of their own destiny.

A fitting conclusion to this chapter is provided by the following account of part of the contemporary South African scene by a character in Nadine Gordimer's novel *Burger's Daughter*, the final sentence of which is as near as prudence permits to a prophecy:

These restless broken streets where definitions fail – the houses the outhouses of white suburbs, two-windows-one-door, multiplied in institutional rows; the hovels with tin lean-tos sheltering huge old American cars blowzy with gadgets; the fancy suburban burglar bars on mean windows of tiny cabins; the roaming children, wolverine dogs, hobbled donkeys, fat naked babies, vagabond chickens and drunks weaving, old men staring, authoritative women shouting, boys in rags, tarts in finery, the smell of offal cooking, the neat patches of mealies between shebeen yards stinking of beer and urine, the litter of twice-discarded possessions, first thrown out by the white man and then picked over by the black – is this conglomerate urban or rural? No electricity in the houses, a telephone an almost impossible luxury: is this a suburb or a strange kind of junk yard? The enormous backyard of the whole white city, where categories and functions lose their ordination and logic . . .

. . . a 'place'; a position whose contradictions those who impose them don't see, and from which will come a resolution they haven't provided for.

Conclusion

The last lines of Nadine Gordimer's portentious evocation of Black South African settlement echo central themes of this book. Place is a position in geographical space located in the history and structure of a society. The various spatial and social relations implicated in a specific place may generate contradictions, the resolution of which provides a motive force for change. What happens may be neither intended by nor welcome to those who plan for particular outcomes. Yet it arises from intentional human action, as individuals and groups respond to, reproduce or seek to alter the structural context of their lives.

Thus, those 'restless broken streets' have a geographical location on the edge of Johannesburg or some such city, which reflects the present structural position of Black labour in the social relations of South Africa and its place in the world economy. The contradictions implicit in the attempt to use spatial organisation so as to acquire Black labour without conceding rights which are usually held to accompany the human embodiment of labour are generating a resolution which increasingly threatens the reproduction of South African society in its present form. The changes which are under way are producing a society significantly different from that planned by the architects of apartheid.

In the United States we have seen how a different kind of capitalist society generates different outcomes. Here place appears not greatly to affect human life chances at the broad regional scale of steady income convergence. Wide divergences exist locally, however, especially within the city, where place in the slums or suburbs is very much a reflection of position in the structure of American society. Planning can restructure urban space, but may exacerbate the geographical reflection of class inequality.

Under socialism also, planning can generate perverse outcomes. The attainment of regional equality in living standards is constrained by spatial selectivity of investment required by efficiency considerations and localisation of natural resources. At the urban scale, within Moscow, residential sorting is giving distinctive spatial expression to inequality, in a city designed to promote equalitarian ideals. Spatial form may feed back into social process, to encourage the further pursuit of localised private self-interest and frustrate the development of true communism.

This book has done little more than scratch the surface of such complexities. But it should at least have opened up a view of the world in which geography and society are mutually interactive elements in the generation of patterns of inequality over the passage of time. Bound each to each in some natural symbiosis, geography and society merge their identity: the one begetting and begotten by the other.

The Child is father of the Man . . .

101

References

Andrusz, G.D. (1984) *Housing and Urban Development in the USSR* (Macmillan, London).

Barbash, N.B. (1983a) 'Nekotorie sotsial'no demograficheskie osobennocti rasselenia v Mockve', *Izvestiya Akademii Nauk SSSR, seriya geograficheska* **1**, 72–81.

Barbash, N.B. (1983b) 'The geographical approach to urban environment-health relationships', *Ecology of Diseases* **2** (2), 117–23.

Barbash, N.B. (1984) 'Otsenka naceleniem uchastov gorodskoi sredi', *Izvestiya Akademii Nauk SSSR, seriya geograficheska* **5**, 81–91.

Barbash, N.B. and Gutnov, A.E. (1980) 'Urban planning aspects of the spatial organisation of Moscow', *Soviet Geography* **11**, 557–73.

Bater, J.H. (1980) *The Soviet City: Ideal and Reality* (Edward Arnold, London).

Bederman S.H. (1974) 'The stratification of "quality of life" in the black community of Atlanta, Georgia', *Southeastern Geographer* **14**(1), 26–37.

Bederman, S.H. and Adams, J. (1974) 'Job accessibility and underemployment', *Annals, Association of American Geographers* **64** (3), 378–86.

Bederman, S.H. and Hartshorn T.A. (1984) 'Quality of life in Georgia: the 1980 experience', *Southeastern Geographer* **24**(2), 78–98.

Browett, J.G. (1980) 'Development and the diffusionist paradigm', *Progress in Human Geography* **4**, 57–79.

Bundy, C. (1986) 'South Africa on the switchback', *New Society*, 3 January, 7–11.

Burman, S. (1979) 'The illusion of progress: race and politics in Atlanta, Georgia', *Ethnic and Racial Studies* **2**(4), 441–54.

Cole, J.P. and Harrison, M.E. (1978) *Regional Inequalities in Services and Purchasing Power in the USSR*, Occasional Paper No. 14 (Department of Geography, Queen Mary College, University of London).

Cutter, S. (1985) *Rating Places, A Geographer's View on Quality of Life* (Association of American Geographers, Washington DC).

Deavers, K.L. (1980) 'Rural conditions and regional differences', Chapter 9 in Arnold, V.L. (ed.) *Alternatives to Confrontation: A National Policy towards Regional Change*, (Lexington Books, Lexington, Mass.).

Drewnowski, J. (1974) *On Measuring and Planning the Quality of Life* (Mouton, The Hague).

Estall, R. (1980) 'The changing balance of the northern and southern regions of the United States', *American Studies* **14**(3), 365–86.

Fair, T.J.D. (1982) *South Africa: Spatial Frameworks for Development* (Juta & Co., Cape Town).

Fox, K. (1978) 'Uneven regional development in the United States', *Review of Radical Political Economics* **10**(3), 68–86.

French, R.A. and Hamilton, F.E.I. (1979) *The Socialist City: Spatial Structure and Urban Policy* (Wiley, Chichester).

Garnick, D.H. and Friedenburg, H.C. (1982) 'Accounting for regional differences in per capita personal income growth, 1929–79', *Survey of Current Business* (US Department of Commerce, Bureau of the Census, September 24–34).

Gore, C. (1984) *Regions in Question: Space Development Theory and Regional Policy* (Methuen, London).

Hall, P. (1984) *The World Cities*, 3rd ed. (Weidenfeld and Nicholson, London).

Hamilton, F.E.I. (1976) *The Moscow City Region*, (Oxford University Press, London).

Hartshorn, T.A., Bederman, S., Davis, S., Dever, G.E.A. and Pillsbury, R. (1976) *Metropolis in Georgia: Atlanta's Rise as a Major Transaction Centre* (Ballinger Publishing Company, Cambridge, Mass.).

Lane, D. (1978) *Politics and Society in the USSR* (Martin Robertson, London).

Massey, D. (1984) *Spatial Divisions of Labour: Social Structure and the Geography of Production* (Macmillan, London).

Morton, H.W. and Stuart, R.C. (1984) *The Contemporary Soviet City* (Macmillan, London).

Nechemias, C. (1980) 'Regional differentiation of living standards in the RSFSR: the issues of inequality', *Soviet Studies* **22**, 366–78.

Omond, R. (1986) *The Apartheid Handbook* (Penguin, Harmondsworth).

Peet, R. (1983) 'Relations of production and the relocation of United States manufacturing industry since 1960', *Economic Geography* **59** (2), 112–43.

Perry, D.C. and Watkins, A.J. (1977) (eds.) *The Rise of the Sunbelt Cities* (Sage Publications, Beverly Hills).

Schiffer, J.R. (1985) 'Interpretations of the issue of "inequality" in Soviet regional policy debates', *International Journal of Urban and Regional Research* **9**(4), 508–32.

Smith, D.M. (1973) *The Geography of Social Well-being in the United States: An Introduction to Territorial Social Indicators* (McGraw-Hill, New York).

Smith, D.M. (1974) 'Who gets what where and how: a welfare focus for human geography', *Geography* **59**, 289–97.

Smith, D.M. (1975) *Patterns in Human Geography: An Introduction to Numerical Methods* (Penguin, Harmondsworth).

Smith, D.M. (1977) *Human Geography: A Welfare Approach* (Edward Arnold, London).

Smith, D.M. (1979) *Where the Grass is Greener: Living in an Unequal World* (Penguin, Harmondsworth).

Smith, D.M. (1981) *Inequality in an American City: Atlanta, Georgia, 1960–1970*, Occasional Paper 17 (Department of Geography, Queen Mary College, University of London).

Smith, D.M. (1982a) 'Inequality in the American and Soviet city: a comparative study of Atlanta and Moscow', in Gray, M. and Lee, R. (eds.) *Fresh Perspectives in Geography*, Special Publications **3**, 1–24 (Department of Geography, Queen Mary College, University of London).

Smith, D.M. (ed.) (1982b) *Living Under Apartheid: Aspects of Urbanization and Social Change in South Africa*, The London Research Series in Geography **2** (Allen & Unwin, London).

Smith, D.M. (1985) *Inequality in Atlanta, Georgia, 1960–1980*, Occasional Paper 25 (Department of Geography and Earth Science, Queen Mary College, University of London).

Smith, D.M. (1987) *Apartheid in South Africa* (Cambridge University Press, Cambridge).

Smith, G (1986) 'Privilege and place in Soviet society', in Gregory D. and Walford R. (eds.) *New Horizons in Human Geography* (Macmillan, London).

Smith, N. (1984) *Uneven Development: Nature, Capital and the Production of Space* (Basil Blackwell, Oxford).

Stone, C.N. (1976) *Economic Growth and Neighbourhood Discontent: System Bias in the Urban Renewal Program of Atlanta* (The University of North Carolina Press, Chapel Hill).

Index